HANNAH'S STORY: YOUR STORY

Lessons from women in the Bible

by

Rev. Dr. Claudette C Rodney

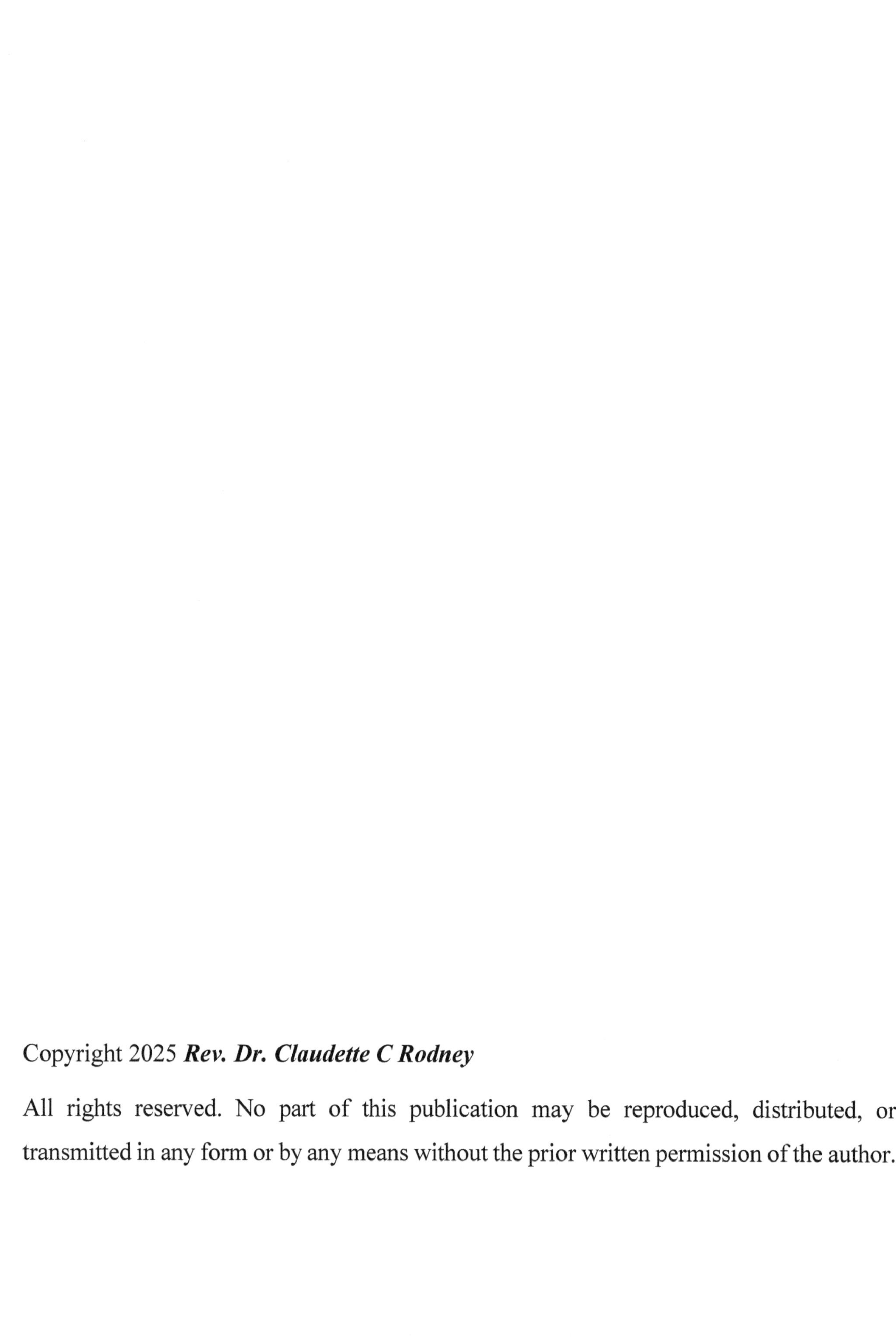

DEDICATION

This book is dedicated first and foremost to my late mother, Hyacinth G. Rodney, who was my biggest supporter and number one fan. I am who I am because of who she was. Thanks, Mom, for all your tough love.

Next, I dedicate this book to all the women in my life; my sisterhood circle; the women who keep me grounded (you know who you are). And especially to my cousin, Lesley Marks Henry (thanks for taking six months away from your family and other obligations to nurse me back to health. I owe a debt that I can never repay). To my bestie, my sister/friend, Lisa Yvette Brown, for providing a safe space for me to grow and be myself. I love you to life!

Last, but not least, this book is dedicated to my nieces, Marcia, JoyAnn, KerriAnn, and Tycia. My godchildren, the late Ayende (gone but not forgotten), Sekelaga, and Nyah, who bring so much joy to my life.

ACKNOWLEDGEMENTS

Initially, I found the inspiration for this book from my dear friend, Dr. Anne LaForte-Moore, who gave me the title *Hannah's Story: Your Story*. She did so after she viewed my initial sermon on videotape.

I would also like to acknowledge Rev. Dr. Herbert D. Daughtry, Bishop Emeritus from the House of the Lord Churches, headquartered in Brooklyn, New York. It was his not-so-subtle nudging that finally got me to move forward and complete this book that began so many years ago.

Without a doubt, I must give all honor and praise to my Lord and Savior, Jesus Christ. Without the Holy Spirit's guidance, none of this would be possible.

ABOUT THE AUTHOR

Rev. Dr. Claudette C. Rodney is a Professional Life Coach and veteran mental health clinician based in Richmond, Virginia. Her aspiration for her platform, Stepping into Destiny LLC, is to provide a "home" for those seeking guidance in life's many challenges and a caring voice amidst the clamor of modern living. As a Certified Professional Life Coach, she empowers her clients to live the life of their dreams. She partners with them to revitalize their relationships, create a balanced work/home life, and stop worrying so they can start living.

Personal: Originally from South America, Dr. Rodney emigrated to the U.S. in her late teens and has amassed a considerable educational, spiritual, and occupational resume.

Educational: Dr. Rodney holds a Doctorate in Psychology from Pace University, New York. An ordained minister of the Gospel of Jesus Christ, Claudette also holds a Master of Divinity from the Samuel DeWitt Proctor School of Theology at Virginia Union University.

Spiritual: A member of The House of the Lord (HOLC) Churches, Rev. Rodney served for 15 years at the congregational headquarters in Brooklyn, New York. In 1989, led by the Spirit of the Lord, Claudette relocated to Beaver Falls, PA, where she served as Church Administrator as well as Youth Advisor for 10 years. In addition, Claudette was also an Associate Minister of the HOLC in Washington, D.C. She now functions as a member and Senior Minister in diaspora.

Occupational/Evangelical:

Dr. Rodney has served in various parts of the U.S., Europe, and Africa as a speaker and consultant. She was selected as an InterFuture Scholar in 1981 and traveled to Ghana, West Africa, and London, England, where she conducted original research on the role of Black Fathers within the Family System, from Ancient Africa to the Modern Day. Through the organization Pan-African Christian Exchange, Claudette participated in two mission trips to Kenya, East Africa. There she served as a psychological consultant to a local Children's Home and the Kiritta School for Children with mental and emotional needs. Rev. Claudette also participated in a mission trip to Uganda, where she ministered in two prisons, a local church, and open-air crusades.

In June 1998, Dr. Rodney presented at the First International Conference on Child & Adolescent Mental Health seminar at the Chinese University of Hong Kong. Her presentation, *PATHWAYS: A Model Service*, is published in *International Perspectives on Child & Adolescent Mental Health*. In 1995, as a psychological consultant, Claudette joined delegates from The House of the Lord Church (Sisters Assisting South Africans) in their exploratory/fact-finding trip to South Africa.

Over the years, Dr. Rodney has gained considerable clinical experience within multi-disciplinary teams, working with children, adolescents, and their families. While at the University of Pittsburgh Medical Center, New Brighton, PA, Dr. Rodney was the Director of Home-Based Family Services. In this role, she provided administrative and clinical supervision to therapists working in-home with multi-problematic families to prevent out-of-home placements of children.

At Greensville Correctional Center in Jarratt, VA, Dr. Rodney was a Psychology Associate Senior for the 1,000 inmates in S3 cluster until her retirement after 18 years. She provided mental health services, including crisis intervention and group psychotherapy, to inmates within the general population.

Rev. Dr. Rodney is also a retired Chaplain with GraceInside, Virginia's Prison Chaplain Service, and Chaplain Supervisor (Central Region). She held positions in the past as an Institutional Chaplain at two large facilities, Chaplain Intern, and Protestant Religious Volunteer. Her duties included monitoring religious programs, sharing the Gospel message, and conducting weekly Bible studies. She has led studies with inmates on Men and Emotions from a Biblical perspective.

Dr. Rodney is enthusiastic about her transition into the role of a Professional Life Coach and helping others navigate the storms of modern life. Her work follows the Gospel of the Lord, who calmed the stormy seas.

CONTENTS

PREFACE

Hey there, Knowledge Seekers!

Welcome, adventurous soul! I'm beyond excited to have you here, flipping through the pages of a journey that has been both thrilling and, at times, downright crazy. This book was birthed from my initial sermon, which I preached in September 2002. Every page you are about to devour is infused with the sparks of inspiration that have struck me like lightning over the years. Trust me, this isn't just another book; it's a treasure map leading you to truths regarding Hannah's story and how it relates to our stories, as well as to the lives of other women in the Bible, such as Ruth, Deborah, Mary, and Esther.

As I began this venture, I had a couple of burning questions in my heart: What can we learn about ourselves from Hannah's story? What fuels the fire within us to persevere even in difficult circumstances? So, armed with an insatiable curiosity, a nudge from the Holy Spirit, and a hefty dose of caffeine, I embarked on a quest to uncover the lessons from the women in the Bible. I delved into countless Bible translations, commentaries, and other relevant books, gathering insights like a squirrel hoarding acorns for winter.

My nights turned into marathons of research; I scribbled notes and filled my walls with colorful post-its that would make any wall come alive! The process was exhilarating, like jumping into a pool of creativity without knowing how deep it was or how cold the water would be! In those moments of exploration, I found the heartbeat of being alive, the essence that makes us human.

I've poured my heart and soul into every chapter, hoping to not just share knowledge but to ignite a spark in you, dear reader. In the pages ahead, expect a whirlwind of stories and metaphors that will knock your socks off! You'll find practical tips that don't just skim the surface; instead, they dive deep into the ocean of revelation and discovery, encouraging you to plunge in headfirst.

Each chapter builds on the last, creating a symphony that celebrates our unique and adaptive survival techniques to the sometimes chaotic rhythm of life. I promise there will be moments that challenge your thinking, push you out of your comfort zone, and inspire you to take leaps of faith! But that's the beauty of this journey, you're not just a bystander; you are a co-creator in this adventure!

So buckle up as we embrace the mistakes, the leaps, and the joyous breakthroughs together! Let's peel back the layers of aversion and fear that hold you back and unleash the dynamic power that resides within you. If this journey fuels your passion and illuminates your path, then I've satisfied my intention. I hope you find joy, laughter, and maybe even a tear or two as we explore the wonderful and messy world of women in society.

Grab a cup of your favorite beverage, get cozy, and let's dive into this fabulous spiritual adventure! Together, let's write a new chapter in the story of our lives.

With gratitude in my heart and a sprinkle of anointing from above.

Rev. Dr. Claudette C. Rodney

HANNAH'S DESPAIR:
A HEART IN THE SHADOWS

Introduction to Hannah's Struggles

In the ancient world, a woman's worth was often measured by her ability to bear children. Within this labyrinth of societal expectations and personal longing, we find Hannah. Her story unfolds against a backdrop steeped in the cultural and familial pressures of motherhood, amplifying the grief and despair that envelop her like a heavy cloak. Hannah is more than just a biblical figure; she symbolizes the silent struggle many women face, both then and now, when they find themselves grappling with the pain of infertility.

Imagine a woman like Hannah in her quiet moments of reflection, sitting in the stillness of her home, the weight of expectation pressing down on her shoulders. Each day brings no relief, only reminders of what she lacks: the laughter of children, the tender coo of a newborn, the warmth of a family gathered together. Instead, she hears the whispers of her community, a chorus of judgment that echoes in the recesses of her heart: "What is wrong with her? Why hasn't she given her husband a child?" These thoughts are not mere echoes; they are daggers that cut deep, creating an ongoing cycle of shame and despair.

In biblical times, the societal role of a woman was deeply intertwined with her capacity to bring forth life. Infertility was not merely a personal struggle but a communal concern, a topic swirling in gossip and innuendo. Hannah's inability to conceive sets her apart from her peers, isolating her in a world that did not understand her heartache. The women in her village, while perhaps sympathetic to her plight, are often quick to judge, blinded by their own understanding of value, children, lineage, and place in society. For Hannah, this scrutiny transforms her social existence into a nightmare where her worth feels irrevocably tied to her ability to conceive.

As she attends gatherings, she observes other women with their children. Each laugh is a reminder of her pain, each coo and giggle a haunting echo of desire unfulfilled. In such moments, feelings of inadequacy blossom within her; these are not just feelings; they are a vivid representation of her longing, a powerful reminder of her perceived failures. Her heart feels like driftwood caught in a raging river, tossed about and battered, yet ever ready to seek the safety of land, solace, and ultimately, acceptance.

Hannah's inner turmoil is exacerbated by Peninnah, her husband Elkanah's other wife, who seems to embody everything Hannah wishes to be. Where Hannah is marked by her silence, Peninnah is vocal and brash, wielding her fertility like a sword in a cruel game of comparison. "Look what I have that you do not," Peninnah taunts, wielding her children as both shield and weapon. Hannah becomes the target of constant reminders that strike at her very identity. Each child Peninnah bears feels like another nail in the coffin of Hannah's self-worth. Each mocking glance received from others reinforces the towering wall of despair encircling her.

Within these hardships, Hannah's relationship with her husband adds another layer of complexity. Elkanah is a loving husband who seeks to comfort her, frequently offering love and reassurance. He calls her by name, a gentle reminder that she is valued for who she is, not merely for what she can provide. Yet, in his efforts to console her, he inadvertently highlights the profound inadequacy she feels regarding the expectations imposed on her. "Am I not more to you than ten sons?" he questions, but this only serves to deepen her ache. It is a tender phrase coated with love, yet it underscores the gap between their realities. The emptiness of Hannah's womb resounds more loudly than his words of affection.

Hannah isolates herself from these realities, retreating into her thoughts, weaving a tapestry of longing and despair. She exists in a dichotomy; while her husband tries to fill the void with love, the world around her seems insatiable in its demands. Each cycle of disappointment builds upon the last, leading Hannah down a dark corridor where hope feels like a distant flicker, often extinguished by the harsh winds of her community's judgment.

As we journey alongside Hannah, it becomes evident that her struggle transcends the physical limitations of infertility. It spirals into an identity crisis, where every day is a confrontation with her perceived failure. Society demands that she find value in motherhood, yet the cruel hands of circumstance refuse to grant her the opportunity to fulfill that role. In this sorrowful silence lies the immense power of her story, a story that resonates across generations, echoing the heartache of those who find themselves in her shoes.

We must also consider the spiritual implications of Hannah's despair. In her culture, motherhood was not only seen as a divine blessing but also as a confirmation of one's standing before God. This belief compounds her suffering, amplifying her feelings of shame and inadequacy. The narrative intersperses secular and spiritual realms, revealing how profoundly intertwined her identity is with her faith. Hannah's longing, not only for children but also to be acknowledged by God, becomes a central theme. This yearning for connection, validation, and ultimately divine intervention underscores the emotional landscape of her life.

Despite her trials, there is a glimmer of resilience within Hannah that begins to emerge in her darkest moments. It hints at an inner strength that refuses to be extinguished, a testament to her indomitable spirit. Even in the shadows of despair, there exists a flicker of hope, an acknowledgment that she cannot drown in her sorrow. While societal pressures aim to suffocate her essence, there is an inherent understanding that deep within her soul lies the potential for transformation. It is this strength that eventually propels her to the temple, where her cries for help ascend toward heaven, a monumental act of faith amidst her turmoil.

As we explore Hannah's struggles, we come to realize that her journey is not singular but reflects a larger, universal experience shared by many women throughout history and today. Infertility, while a deeply personal experience, reverberates within the community, culture, and even faith, creating ripples that touch countless lives. Hannah invites us to step into her story, to walk alongside her through the valley of despair, and to understand that her pain, while uniquely hers, finds resonance in the hearts of many.

Through understanding Hannah's emotional landscape, readers are encouraged to reflect on their struggles and the societal expectations they may face. In Hannah, we see not just a figure from antiquity but a mirror reflecting our own fears, desires, and hopes. Her life beckons us to uncover the layers of our own identity, revealing the threads of despair woven into the fabric of our existence. In exploring Hannah's story, we begin the important work of empathy, recognizing that vulnerability connects us in ways that transcend time and space.

In her desperation, Hannah teaches us that our struggles do not diminish us; instead, they can catalyze profound transformation. Her faith in the face of despair becomes a beacon, urging us to seek solace beyond the shadows, reminding us that even in our darkest hours, there is grace to be found. The exploration of Hannah's emotional landscape ultimately invites us to embrace our own stories; to acknowledge our vulnerabilities and to celebrate the journey each person embarks on in pursuit of fulfillment, identity, and hope.

The Weight of Expectations

Hannah's story resonates deeply, not only in its historical context but also in its exploration of the expectations placed upon women, a theme that remains relevant today. The weight of societal and familial expectations can often feel unbearable, particularly for women who navigate the complex landscape of identity, worth, and societal roles. Just as Hannah faced the painful pressure of motherhood and its implications in her patriarchal society, women today often find themselves grappling with similar expectations that shape their lives in profound ways.

In the biblical narrative, Hannah is characterized by her anguish and desperation. She is a woman who longs for a child in a society where motherhood is closely intertwined with a woman's identity and value. The inability to bear children not only affects her personal happiness but also her status within her family and community. In Hannah's time, motherhood was not simply a desire but an expectation. A woman without children risked not only her fulfillment but her very identity, as much of her worth was tied to her ability to bear heirs. This cultural backdrop serves as a poignant reminder of how societal expectations can define and often confine women's lives.

Today, while the context may have evolved, the essence of these expectations remains. Women are often expected to fulfill multiple roles, caregivers, professionals, nurturers, and more, while balancing the pursuit of their individuality. The societal pressure to conform to these roles can create a sense of inadequacy for those who struggle to meet these expectations. For many, the challenge becomes not just about achieving success in these roles but also about reconciling personal aspirations with the weight of societal norms. The success narratives that flood the media often present an idealized version of womanhood, one that may not feel attainable for all.

Hannah's anguish in the temple serves as an emotional focal point in her story. She pours out her heart to God, expressing her pain and longing. This vulnerability resonates with many women who have felt their worth dictated by external circumstances. In her desperate prayer, Hannah exemplifies the struggle for self-identity amidst societal pressures. She does not merely seek a child; she seeks to restore her value and dignity as a woman. This inner turmoil is echoed in the voices of contemporary women who grapple with similar feelings of inadequacy, whether stemming from career ambitions, relationships, or societal ideals of success.

Taking inspiration from Hannah's plea, women today are challenged to navigate the landscape of their identities and worth. The modern-day woman often finds herself negotiating between personal desires and commonly held expectations from families and society. The cultural implications of motherhood extend beyond the biblical narrative, influencing how women view their choices and the paths available to them. For some, the pressure to have children can feel overwhelming, leading to feelings of grief or inadequacy, similar to what Hannah experienced. Moreover, societal narratives often equate a woman's success with her ability to fulfill traditional roles. This type of thinking breeds a narrow definition of success, one that can marginalize those who do not conform to established ideals, such as childlessness by choice, single motherhood, or prioritizing career achievements over family life.

The juxtaposition of Hannah's story against modern societal expectations amplifies the conversation surrounding the worth and identity of women. Hannah's relationship with Peninnah, the other wife in her household, adds another layer to the expectations placed upon women. Peninnah, who had children, served as a constant reminder of Hannah's perceived failure. Her antagonism illustrates how women can become competitors within their own gender, vying for validation and recognition in a world that often sets them against one another. This dynamic of comparison continues today; women frequently find themselves measuring their worth against that of others, whether through social media portrayals of "perfect" lives or workplace competition.

In Hannah's time, a woman's identity was largely defined by her role as a mother. This cultural standard echoes throughout history and remains influential in countless cultures around the world. The societal belief that a woman's primary purpose is to bear children can lead to significant pressure, creating a painful divide between personal choice and community expectation. Hannah's despair encapsulates this tension; her dreams of motherhood serve as a window into the bigger picture of womanhood that transcends her individual experience.

Throughout Hannah's narrative, her eventual triumph in being granted a child is a turning point that also deserves deeper reflection. While her circumstances change with the birth of Samuel, the underlying issue of identity and worth does not simply vanish. Her journey highlights the complexity of reconstituting one's value within a context that often equates success with external achievements. The birth of Samuel, although a joyous occasion, does not erase the years of pain and struggle that preceded it.

Similarly, in contemporary dialogues about womanhood, the idea of success is often too closely linked with milestones such as marriage or motherhood. Many women find their worth being questioned when they diverge from this path. Voices advocating for broader definitions of success emphasize the need to recognize accomplishments beyond traditional benchmarks. By embracing a more inclusive understanding of womanhood that values individual choices and experiences, society begins to dismantle the restrictive narratives that have historically contributed to women's feelings of worthlessness or despair when they do not fit the mold.

In examining contemporary voices and narratives, one can uncover a wealth of experiences that bear resemblance to Hannah's. Stories of women who have faced infertility, chosen to pursue their careers over traditional roles, or found peace in alternative family structures are profound and varied. These narratives challenge the status quo and enlarge the definition of womanhood, underscoring that identity and worth are not singular nor static. The weight of expectations can become lighter when women uplift one another and share their diverse stories. Creating spaces for dialogue around the complexities of womanhood, the struggle for balance, and the battle against societal norms allows for healing and growth. By advocating for each individual's narrative, women can find strength in vulnerability and discernment in their unique journeys.

As we draw parallels between Hannah's story and contemporary challenges faced by women, it becomes evident that her anguish serves as a precursor to liberation. While the societal pressures to fulfill predetermined roles remain, Hannah's ultimate cry for help culminates in divine intervention and personal transformation. Through her experience, women are reminded that it is their desire, struggle, and voice that truly shape their identities and worth.

Ultimately, Hannah's narrative acts as a reflection of the resilience and complexity inherent in every woman's journey. By acknowledging and validating personal experiences, we can challenge the expectations imposed upon women and foster a greater understanding of the myriad ways to define success, identity, and worth in our modern world. The story of Hannah encourages women to embrace their unique paths, to seek their voices, and to find solace in their individuality, regardless of societal expectations.

In conclusion, the weight of expectations can be a heavy burden, but it can also catalyze growth and transformation. By examining Hannah's despair and her path toward hope, we find a powerful message for women today: that while society may place pressures on our identities, we have the capacity to redefine our worth through resilience, community, and authentic self-expression. The journey of self-discovery is deeply personal, and it is through sharing and learning from one another that we can begin to lift the weight of expectations and embrace the fullness of our stories. As we step into our identities and worth, may we echo Hannah's cry and find strength in our struggles, illuminating the path toward healing and transformation for ourselves and the women who walk alongside us.

Silent Suffering and Divine Absence

In the quiet corners of Hannah's heart, where hope dared to linger and despair loomed large, there lay an enduring struggle, the experience of divine silence amid deep suffering. Her story, woven into the very fabric of biblical history, is one of anguish, longing, and a steadfast quest for meaning in the face of overwhelming adversity. In the echoes of her cries, modern women find resonance, as many navigate their own silent battles, struggling to make sense of their pain in a world that seems indifferent.

Hannah, the fervent mother of Samuel, stands as a symbol of the anguished soul longing for recognition and relief. Her journey starts in a place most women can understand: yearning for the blessing of motherhood in a culture that places immense value on reproduction. She endured taunts and barbs slung by her rival, Peninnah, who mothered children with ease while Hannah remained barren, consumed by the shadow of her inadequacy. Yet, the depths of her suffering were not merely social; they were profoundly spiritual. Hannah cried out to God, her prayers filled with anguish, but in return, she often encountered silence, a divine absence that would bring any believer to their knees.

How does one reconcile the silence of God with the depth of their suffering? This is the crux of Hannah's despair. She offered her heartfelt supplications year after year, pouring out her soul to the Lord within the sacred confines of the temple. "O Lord of hosts," she pleaded, "if you will indeed look on the affliction of your servant and remember me." In that moment, Hannah embodies the struggle many face when it seems that heaven has turned a deaf ear to their pleas. The feeling of divine silence is a paradox of faith, a testing ground that shakes the very foundations of belief. It raises questions that ripple through the ages: Why does God seem close to some yet distant from others? Is there a purpose behind the silence? For Hannah, as for many modern women, the cry for help in solitude becomes an act of courage and vulnerability. How many of us, like Hannah, find ourselves standing in the shadows of our pain, sobbing into the void, hoping that someone, anyone, might hear?

Silent suffering is a profound experience, often compounded by the expectation of resilience. Society can sometimes demand that we wear a mask of strength, that we carry our burdens in solitude, pretending everything is all right when inside, turmoil rages. Hannah's boldness in revealing her pain stands as a radical act in a world that often prioritizes stoicism over vulnerability. In her silence, she found the courage to voice her pain, praying fervently even when it felt as though no one was listening. Imagine the depths of her sorrow as she witnessed Peninnah's children, tangible symbols of abundance and fulfillment, while her own empty arms ached for what society deemed the ultimate validation of womanhood. It was not just the lack of children that pained her; it was the societal perception that accompanied it. Each month that passed carried the weight of shame, failure, and loneliness. As she visited the temple to pray, the echo of her anguish reverberated in the rafters, perhaps unanswered but undeniably sincere.

In our fast-paced, modern world, the silence can often feel amplified. Women today navigate a myriad of roles: caregivers, professionals, nurturers, all while facing challenges both internal and external. There are moments when life's burdens feel insurmountable, and the desperation that drips into prayer seems to go unnoticed. Women share stories of battling infertility, career obstacles, personal loss, and societal pressures, often feeling as though their cries for help are lost in the ether.

It is easy to feel abandoned during these times. When prayers go unanswered, grief and confusion can fester, leading to disillusionment. Just as Hannah stood before Eli, the priest, poured out her heart, and was misunderstood, labeled as drunk when she was merely desperate, modern women often find their struggles minimized or dismissed. The responses can range from well-meaning but misguided advice to outright disbelief. We must ask ourselves: How often do we respond to the struggles of others with the same misunderstanding that Hannah faced? For every Hannah who has felt unheard in her suffering, there is an opportunity for empathy. The church, historically a stronghold of community, can sometimes become a place where silent suffering is overlooked or inadequately addressed. Women who gather for fellowship may share stories of triumphs but regard their struggles as weaknesses to be hidden. Yet, Hannah's story calls us to embrace the entirety of our experiences, including the shadows. Silence can be deafening, yet it is in these quiet places that God often prepares us for what is ahead.

In Hannah's case, her silence led to a profound encounter with the divine. After years of anguish, the moment came when she heard Eli's words: "Go in peace, and the God of Israel grant your petition." The flicker of hope ignited a response within her, the faith that she would indeed have a child. This faith was not some naïve gloss over her pain; instead, it was a raw acknowledgment that a spirit deep within her recognized the possibility of change.

The divine silence Hannah experienced was not a rejection but rather an invitation. It beckoned her deeper into her faith, challenging her to cling to hope even when the odds seemed insurmountable. Similarly, modern women can find empowerment in those moments of silence, not as a sign of abandonment but as an opportunity for introspection, transformation, and ultimately, a reorientation of faith. Hannah's joy upon Samuel's birth was not just the culmination of her prayers; it was a testament to her journey through despair, building strength through her silent suffering.

Hannah's story teaches us that enduring through silence can lead to profound revelations about ourselves and our connection with God. Many contemporary women might share their journeys through despair while holding onto fleeting moments of faith. In the silence, we confront our fears and doubts, but we also cultivate resilience and an unwavering spirit. It is vital to remember that our prayers, no matter how desperate, are never wasted. In the depths of our battles, God is present, often in ways we may not immediately perceive.

Consider the women who silently suffer in our own lives. Each one carries an unseen story of turmoil. Their exteriors may project calmness, while internally they wrestle with unanswered prayers and the weight of the world. They may, like Hannah, retreat into prayer, their hearts beating against the walls of expectation and heartache. The church and community must strive to be places where women can voice their struggles without fear of judgment. Just as Hannah found a voice in her suffering, we must encourage others to speak their truth.

In worship settings, the practice of lament can unveil the raw humanity that we all share. We can learn from Hannah's fierce honesty in bringing her anguish before God, creating safe spaces for private pain to be acknowledged within communal worship. Together, may we support one another through the valleys of despair by holding space for both the struggles and the successes. As these reflections unfurl, we must hold onto the knowledge that Hannah's story does not end in silence. Her subsequent prayers, propelled by faith, resulted in the birth of Samuel, a prophet whose life would significantly alter the course of Israel's history. In moments of divine absence, there is often the anticipation of divine presence waiting to be revealed. The silence is potent; it is a teacher of endurance, patience, and profound faith. For Hannah, it cultivated a heart that could one day hold immense gratitude. There, in the fullness of her experience of longing and fulfillment, secular ideas of success faded in the presence of divine purpose.

As we traverse the terrain of silence together, may we honor our struggles while seeking connection and understanding. In the shadows of Hannah's despair, let us also seek the light, knowing that through the silence of our suffering, God writes a story not just for us but through us. In that unfolding narrative, may we continue to strive for connection, empathy, and an unwavering spirit, echoing Hannah's truth through our own lives.

THE POWER OF PRAYER: WHISPERING HOPES

The Essence of Hannah's Prayer

Hannah's story is often remembered for her extraordinary faith and the miraculous birth of her son, Samuel, but the heart of her narrative lies deeply intertwined with the essence of her prayers. When we delve into the structure and emotional depth of Hannah's prayers, we uncover layers of raw vulnerability and profound longing for connection with God. Her prayers are not mere words; they are the very pulse of her being, a reflection of her innermost struggles, desires, and hopes.

From the very beginning of her story, we see Hannah steeped in a life marked by sorrow. Barren and tormented by the taunts of Peninnah, her husband Elkanah's other wife, she found herself ensnared in the agony of unmet expectations and societal pressures. In a culture where motherhood was paramount, Hannah's barrenness was not just a personal grief; it was a public shame. Yet, amid this turmoil, she chose prayer as her haven. Her prayers are raw and sincere, stripped of pretense and facade. In her moments of despair, she does not shy away from expressing her anguish before God.

Hannah's prayer is both a heartfelt cry and a structured plea, woven together in a manner that captures the essence of her relationship with the divine. The depth of her emotions is evident in her choice of language and posture. First and foremost, she approaches God with a deep sense of humility. She acknowledges her brokenness and helplessness, recognizing her inability to change her circumstances. This humility is foundational to her prayer life; it sets the tone for her petitions and gives weight to her requests.

"Lord Almighty, if you will only look upon your servant's misery and remember me," she pleads in 1 Samuel 1:11. In these words, we see not only a request for a son but a yearning for acknowledgment. It is a plea for recognition of her suffering and a desire for God's intervention in her life. Hannah does not simply want a child; she longs to be seen by God, to be heard in her pain. This notion of being remembered is a recurring theme in the Bible, often associated with divine favor and intervention. Hannah's prayer is rich with this longing, revealing her deep desire for connection.

The emotional depth of Hannah's prayer intensifies as she articulates not just her desire for a child but also her promise to dedicate him to the Lord's service. This vow encapsulates the sacrificial nature of her request. In her anguish, she does not merely seek a blessing for herself but envisions a legacy that glorifies God. Her commitment signifies a turning point in her relationship with God; it transforms her prayer from a mere expression of need into an act of worship and devotion.

The significance of prayer as a tool for emotional release in Hannah's life cannot be overstated. In her anguish, she finds solace in the act of pouring out her heart to God. The emotional weight she carries is released through her prayers, allowing her to confront her grief head-on. The act of praying becomes therapeutic, offering her a safe space to be honest about her feelings and struggles. It is in this sacred exchange that she finds the strength to navigate her turmoil. The narrative illustrates how prayer serves as a conduit for emotional release, an opportunity to confront pain, seek comfort, and ultimately find hope.

Hannah's posture during prayer is also telling. In 1 Samuel 1:12-13, we find her praying silently, her lips moving but her voice unheard. This image reverberates with a sense of desperation and intimacy. Silence in prayer often speaks louder than words; it reveals a depth of connection that transcends verbal communication. Hannah's silent prayer reflects the intensity of her feelings, highlighting that sometimes, in times of deepest sorrow, words may fail us. The essence of prayer rests not only in articulating requests but also in yielding our hearts in the quiet presence of God.

As Hannah's story unfolds, we see the transformation that prayer brings to her life. After she prays, her demeanor shifts noticeably. Eli, the priest, notices her changing spirit and even interprets her earnestness as drunkenness, a misunderstanding that underscores the depth of her emotional experience. Yet, it is through this encounter that Hannah finds affirmation. Eli's blessing serves as confirmation of her prayers and hopes. When her emotional burdens are lifted through prayer, she is able to leave the temple with a newfound sense of peace. This profound shift emphasizes a vital aspect of prayer: its power to transform our inner state, to turn sorrow into hope, and despair into faith.

The experience of Hannah teaches us that prayer is not merely about receiving answers but is an essential form of communication with the divine. It fosters a relationship built on intimacy, trust, and vulnerability. Hannah's story invites us to reflect on our own prayer lives. Are we bringing our full selves to the table? Are we expressing our raw emotions, or are we cloaked in pretense? Are we willing to expose our vulnerabilities before God, much like Hannah did?

Moreover, the essence of Hannah's prayer encourages us to remember that our needs are valid in the eyes of God. Whether our cries are for healing, provision, or connection, we are invited to voice them freely. Hannah's journey illustrates that our most profound moments of prayer often arise from our deepest wounds. It is through these moments that we allow God to enter our struggles and transform them into opportunities for growth.

As we examine Hannah's prayer more deeply, we can identify key components that make it an exemplary model of sincere dialogue with the Almighty. First, there is honesty. Hannah does not sugarcoat her pain; she lays it bare before God. Second, there is specificity. She is clear about what she wants; she asks for a son. Third, there is commitment. Hannah makes a vow that entwines her desires with God's will, signifying her depth of devotion. Together, these components create a template for prayer that resonates throughout the ages. As contemporary women often grapple with their own versions of barrenness, whether emotional, spiritual, or relational, Hannah's approach to prayer serves as a beacon of hope. It exemplifies the importance of being honest in our prayers, not shying away from articulating our fears and aspirations. We learn that vulnerability is not weakness; rather, it is a powerful catalyst for connection with God. Whether we are battling societal pressures, personal grief, or spiritual doubt, we find in Hannah's story the assurance that prayer holds the key to unlocking our deepest desires and releasing our burdens.

In the tapestry of Biblical narratives, Hannah's prayer stands as a testament to the transformative power of connecting with God through prayer. It reveals the tender dance between human longing and divine grace. As she pours out her heart in anguish, she receives not just the desire of her heart but the strength to continue in faith, reminding us that God meets us at our place of need, calling us to cast our cares upon Him.

Prayer, as illustrated by Hannah's experience, is not merely a set of requests or a ritual to be practiced. It is a life-giving dialogue that has the potential to heal, restore, and rejuvenate our spirits. As we draw near to God in prayer, we, too, can echo the sentiments of Hannah: a blend of suffering, supplication, and surrender that opens the door to divine intervention and unfolds the story of our lives with all its complexities.

In conclusion, the essence of Hannah's prayer is characterized by its emotional depth, vulnerability, and transformative power. Through her example, we are encouraged to embrace our own prayers with authenticity and commitment, trusting that God listens and responds. As we journey through our lives, may we find the courage to whisper our hopes, fears, and regrets to the One who not only hears us but longs for a relationship with us, a relationship that, like Hannah's, can shape our destinies and fulfill our deepest longings.

Transformational Moments in Prayer

In the journey of faith peeved throughout the Bible, few paths shine as brightly as the story of Hannah. Her narrative is one of desperation, fervent faith, and unwavering prayer, culminating in a transformational moment that not only altered her life but also changed the course of Israel's history. Prayer for her was not merely a ritualistic recital of requests but a heartfelt dialogue with God, imbued with passion and raw emotion. This chapter explores the specific instances of divine intervention in response to heartfelt prayer, revealing how Hannah's story serves as an exemplary model of persistence and faith for contemporary believers.

To understand the depth of Hannah's transformative moments in prayer, we must first examine the circumstances that drove her to her knees. Hannah, the wife of Elkanah, grappled with the heavy burden of infertility in a culture that equated a woman's worth with her ability to bear children. The pain of having her rival, Peninnah, continually provoking her about her barrenness intensified Hannah's anguish. It is within this context of deep sorrow and yearning that her prayers emerged, not from a place of routine or obligation, but from the depths of her broken heart.

One pivotal moment in Hannah's journey took place at Shiloh, where she went to pray in the temple. Both profound desperation and an earnest commitment to faith marked this moment. Scripture recounts that Hannah, in her distress, "wept bitterly" and poured out her soul to the Lord. This image is powerful; it is not just prayer in the traditional sense, but a raw expression of vulnerability and a plea for divine intervention. It was the moment when her prayers transcended mere words and transformed into an act of surrender to God's will.

Hannah's petition was specific: she prayed for a son, vowing that if God granted her this desire, she would dedicate him to the Lord for his entire life. Such boldness in prayer not only illustrates her desperation but also her profound faith in God's sovereignty. This duality of heartbreak and hope reveals a core lesson for contemporary believers: that our prayers can be deeply personal and yet aligned with God's purposes. It challenges us to express our true desires to God, trusting that our vulnerability is met with divine compassion.

The transformative power of Hannah's prayer was met with an immediate divine response. Eli, the priest, initially misinterpreted her fervent prayer as drunkenness, yet upon realizing her sincerity, he blessed her. Eli's blessing served as a moment of affirmation and assurance that Hannah's prayers had been heard. It is an important reminder that sometimes divine intervention is mediated through others, particularly those placed in our lives for encouragement and discernment. Hannah's moment of reassurance through Eli's words highlights the communal aspects of prayer and the ways God works through the body of believers.

After this encounter, Hannah left the temple with a changed heart. The Scriptures state, "Then she went her way and ate something, and her face was no longer downcast." This moment is transformational, showcasing how an encounter with God in prayer can shift not just circumstances but also our inner realities. Hope replaced despair, and this interior transformation prepared her for what was to come. When we engage in authentic prayer, we, too, can experience this shift, a movement from hopelessness to faith, from anxiety to assurance.

As Hannah's story continues, she eventually conceived and bore a son, Samuel, fulfilling her vow to God. This outcome not only marked a personal victory but also had significant implications for the Israelites, as Samuel would grow to be a great prophet and leader. The narrative demonstrates that prayer can catalyze transformations that reach far beyond our personal circumstances, impacting our communities and the generations to come. Hannah's experience teaches us that God's answers to prayer are often woven into a larger tapestry that includes His broader purposes in the world.

In contemporary contexts, the lessons gleaned from Hannah's story remain ever relevant. People today navigate a multitude of struggles, whether they be relational, professional, or personal. Much like Hannah, we may find ourselves crying out for help, yearning for God's intervention in our lives. The first practical application is to encourage believers to articulate their prayers authentically and with specificity, just as Hannah did. When we approach God with our burdens, it is vital to shed the notion that our prayers need to be polished or conventional. Hannah's example teaches us the importance of honesty in prayer. This requires a willingness to be truly seen by God, to bring our fears and hopes into the light. Practicing such transparency can lead to a deeper relationship with God, paving the way for transformative encounters.

Moreover, the power of intercessory prayer emerges from Hannah's narrative as another vital lesson. Hannah's prayer was driven not only by her personal need. In dedicating her son to the Lord, she became part of the divine plan for Israel. In contemporary practice, this invites believers to lift others in prayer, expanding their perspective and deepening their communal bonds. When we suffer, it is easy to become wholly absorbed in our pain, yet Hannah's story reminds us of the power of communal intercession. Engaging in prayer for others fosters connections and invites divine action on behalf of those in need.

In addition, recognizing the role of spiritual mentorship in prayer is another essential aspect to draw from Hannah's life. Eli's role in affirming Hannah's prayers showed how vital it is to have figures in our lives who can encourage and support our faith journeys. Just as Eli acted as a spiritual guide, so too must contemporary believers seek out and also become mentors to those around them. In doing so, we create communities filled with accountability, support, and encouragement that reinforce the transformative power of prayer.

Prayerful waiting is another critical lesson gleaned from Hannah's life. After her passionate supplication, there was a season of waiting before she received God's answer. This interval is often fraught with challenges, as we grapple with doubt and impatience. However, it is during these moments that our faith deepens and matures. Engaging actively in waiting, remaining hopeful and steadfast, teaches us reliance on God's perfect timing. As we cultivate patience, our character is refined, and we become more aligned with God's will.

Finally, Hannah's dedication of Samuel to God serves as a profound reminder of the outcomes that follow transformative prayer. When experiencing answered prayers, believers are called to respond with gratitude and commitment. In our fast-paced culture, it can be easy to move quickly from asking to receiving, but Hannah's vow reminds us of the importance of acknowledging God's faithfulness and the necessity of our commitment to God's plans. Just as she dedicated Samuel, we are invited to dedicate our lives, talents, and outcomes to the Lord, ensuring that we recognize the source of our blessings.

As we reflect on the narrative of Hannah and the rich lessons embedded within her story, we see that prayer is more than merely a request; it is a vehicle for transformation that can renew our spirit, realign our focus, and open avenues for divine intervention. In a world filled with distractions and uncertainties, Hannah's example offers timeless wisdom: when we approach God with sincerity and a willingness to be transformed, we become part of a sacred dialogue that shapes not only our futures but the futures of those around us.

In conclusion, the transformational moments in prayer captured through Hannah's life echo across the centuries, reminding us of the potent blend of vulnerability, persistence, and faith. As we engage in prayer, let us embrace the raw honesty of our hearts combined with unwavering hope in God's plans. Through prayer, may we find renewed strength, a deeper connection to God, and an increased ability to intercede for others, ultimately participating in the broader tapestry of God's purpose. Each whisper of hope becomes a powerful testament to God's faithfulness, echoing in our lives as a legacy of faith for generations to come.

Community and Collective Prayer

In the tapestry of life, the threads of community and collective prayer weave together in intricate patterns, creating a support system that can uplift and sustain individuals through the trials and tribulations they face. Hannah's journey, marked by heartache and fervent prayer, reveals the profound impact a supportive community can have on one's faith and healing. As we delve into the role of community in Hannah's life, we discover how collective prayer not only nurtured her spirit but also fostered connections that paralleled her experiences, ultimately leading to strength and resilience in her journey.

From the very outset, Hannah found herself in a challenging environment. She was one among many in a family dynamic fraught with competition and emotional turmoil. The scriptures introduce us to her as a woman deeply troubled by her inability to conceive, a source of pain exacerbated by the taunts of her rival, Peninnah. This rivalry was not merely a personal affliction; it was a communal display of conflict within a family unit that extended beyond Hannah and Peninnah to the broader community around them. Hannah's pain echoed throughout her household, yet it was within that same community that the seeds of support and collective prayer began to take root.

Hannah's journey to Shiloh serves as a significant turning point in understanding the power of communal faith. When she arrived at the temple, burdened with despair, she did not isolate herself; instead, she poured out her soul before the Lord in earnest prayer. It was here, in her vulnerability, that she assumed an important role within the communal context of worship. The act of prayer, particularly within a public and shared space, became a statement of faith that transcended her individual struggles. Her silent, yet fervent, prayers resonated not only with the Lord but also echoed within the hearts of those present.

The role of the high priest, Eli, further exemplifies the collective responsibility woven within prayer. His initial misunderstanding of Hannah's actions reveals a deeper truth about community: often, the most significant moments occur in the intersection between personal expression and communal interpretation. Eli's eventual blessing of Hannah acted as a profound acknowledgment of her pain and faith, creating a bridge of connection that linked their individual experiences. In this moment, Hannah's prayer became not just her own but a part of a larger narrative woven by their shared faith in God. Eli's involvement signified that, in the journey of faith, participation and acknowledgment by others are vital components for healing.

The sacred space of the temple acted as more than just a physical structure; it was a communal hub where prayers were lifted, hopes were shared, and burdens were collectively borne. This underscores the importance of having a community that recognizes individual struggles and collectively engages in prayer. In Hannah's case, she stepped into a shared space where others also gathered with their requests, doubts, and thanksgiving. Each prayer, whether vocalized or silent, contributed to a collective energy aimed at uplifting one another, creating a dynamic atmosphere that invited God's presence into their midst.

As we reflect on the importance of community in Hannah's story, we notice that she did not walk her path alone. The support from those in the temple allowed her to process her grief in a space steeped in faith. Collective prayer served as a balm to her wounds, reinforcing the notion that she was not the solitary bearer of pain. In a world that often seeks to divide individuals, Hannah's experience reminds us of the vital connections created through communal faith practices.

Moreover, prayer within a community fosters resilience. It encourages individuals to be vulnerable, share their stories, and support one another. Just as Hannah found solace in the gathering at Shiloh, we, too, can find strength in the collective voices of those who pray with us. When one person lifts their voice in prayer, it has the power to uplift many. The act of praying together not only reinforces relationships, but can also catalyze healing and restoration. Students, pastors, friends, and family members can unite their faith in communal prayer, where every whisper of hope is interconnected, creating a powerful response to life's challenges.

Consider the influence of shared stories within a community. When Hannah's story was shared, it resonated deeply with the women around her who might have experienced similar struggles. The act of sharing testimonies, whether of pain or answered prayers, not only builds empathy but also fortifies the faith of others. Each testimony becomes a reminder of God's faithfulness and prompts further collective prayer, allowing the community to rally around each other and bear burdens together.

Additionally, Hannah's story encourages us to bring communal faith practices into our lives actively. Establishing prayer circles, church groups, or community events centered around prayer can create environments where individuals feel valued and supported. When we commit to gathering intentionally in collective prayer, we expand the realization that we are not alone. It's essential to create spaces in our lives where people can freely express their hopes, fears, and desires.

Modern examples abound, illustrating the transformative power of collective prayer in a community. Consider the phenomenon of prayer groups in churches or online communities where individuals across distances unite in prayer for one another. These gatherings serve as a unifying force, drawing people together, breaking down barriers, and fostering a sense of belonging. People tap into the collective energy generated by shared prayer, allowing it to carry them through their struggles, just as the faith of her community surrounded Hannah.

Throughout history, we see how communal prayer has played pivotal roles in the lives of believers. The early church, for instance, exemplified the power of communal engagement through prayer. Acts of the Apostles recounts how believers gathered regularly in prayer, seeking the presence of the Holy Spirit and interceding for one another. Such practices not only strengthened their faith but also fortified their community against the challenges they faced.

When we take cues from Hannah's experience, we realize that finding strength in communal faith is not merely about seeking personal relief; it's about participating in a larger story of divine love and support. Our individual struggles and prayers contribute to a greater legacy, one that echoes the consistency of God's goodness over time and motivates others to engage in prayer as well.

While Hannah faced deep sorrow, her story culminates in joy and fulfillment. After her fervent prayer and the blessing of Eli, she eventually bore a son, Samuel, dedicating him to the Lord in gratitude. This act of thanksgiving toward the community reflects the culmination of support that Hannah received throughout her journey. Her response is an invitation for us to recognize the power of community; when we uplift each other in prayer, we contribute not only to others' journeys but also to our own.

As we navigate the complexities of our modern lives filled with challenges and uncertainties, reflecting on Hannah's experiences empowers us to recognize the transformational potential found within our communities. By engaging in collective prayer, we develop a web of support that upholds us. It calls us to be vulnerable, to voice our struggles, and to invite others into our battles, fostering connections that can mirror the truth experienced in communal worship.

In closing, let us remember that Hannah's story is not merely about her personal struggles but also about the intricate web of community that surrounded her. Her transformation through prayer resonates within the hearts of believers today, encouraging us to embrace collective prayer as a powerful tool for healing and connection. Let us gather, share our stories, lift our voices in unity, and allow prayer to intertwine our lives in faith and love as we navigate our own journeys. In the whispers of our hopes, may we find strength in one another, reflecting the boundless grace and support found in community.

PENINNAH'S CHALLENGE: THE BITTER BLOSSOMS OF RIVALRY

The Nature of Rivalry

In the quiet spaces of biblical narratives, the relationships between women often reveal a depth of emotion and complexity that resonates throughout generations. Among these stories, the dynamic between Hannah and Peninnah stands as a poignant example of rivalry, envy, and the painful blossoms they bring. In examining their intertwined lives, we uncover the layers of ambition, pain, and conflict that define not only their relationship but the broader human experience of rivalry.

At the heart of this narrative is Peninnah, a woman whose existence seemed overshadowed by her counterpart, Hannah. While Peninnah bore children, something that society held as a sign of favor and success, Hannah struggled with infertility, which rendered her feelings of inadequacy even sharper. The silence of Hannah's womb echoed loudly in a culture that celebrated motherhood as the highest achievement for women. In such an environment, Peninnah's children were not merely symbols of her success; they were instruments of rivalry wielded to further unsettle Hannah's already fragile sense of worth.

Peninnah's motivations become a focal point when dissecting their rivalry. Was her hostility born from a natural desire to defend her own position in a household where competition was inevitable, or did deeper insecurities fuel it? Despite her apparent triumph in bearing children, Peninnah may have felt threatened by Hannah's worth in the eyes of Elkanah, her husband. Mothers are often viewed as nurturers, but Peninnah's actions suggest a different kind of maternal instinct, one fraught with the need for validation. She became a rival not just to win Elkanah's affection but perhaps to quell her own insecurities about being enough in a world that measured women's worth by their ability to bear children.

The hallway of their shared home became a stage for profound emotional turmoil. Peninnah's taunts were not merely cruel jabs; they were a reflection of her inner turmoil. In essence, Peninnah's rivalry with Hannah reveals a truth about human relationships: the need to feel superior often masks deeper feelings of inferiority. Her mocking words created a tapestry of pain, ensnaring both women in a web of jealousy and sorrow. Each insult heaped upon Hannah was likely laced with Peninnah's own fears: fear of being unloved despite her motherhood, fear that she was not truly secure in Elkanah's affections, and fear that her position could easily be threatened if Hannah were to become successful in having children of her own.

On the other hand, Hannah's response to Peninnah's relentless taunts is both telling and tragic. Rather than retaliate with equal venom or jealousy, Hannah chooses a different path. Her initial silence reflects the weight of her pain, a pain laced with the bitterness of rivalry. Often, when faced with mockery, individuals can lash out in anger, but Hannah's choice to retreat into herself reveals a deeper strength. Instead of succumbing to envy, she turns her heart toward God. In the face of ridicule, Hannah seeks solace not in her husband's love but in her faith. This response offers a significant lesson for readers today: in the throes of rivalry, turning inward or seeking divine assistance can provide a path to healing rather than perpetuating a cycle of bitterness.

While Hannah's actions speak to her resilience and faithfulness, it is crucial to address the complexity of her circumstances. Her silence not only reflects strength but acknowledges the painful truth of her rivalry with Peninnah. In many ways, Hannah embodies the silent struggle of women who navigate competitive relationships, often feeling unworthy despite their inherent value. By opening up to God, she sets an example for women today, encouraging them to communicate their pain and ask not for mere victory over rivals, but for recognition of their worth in the eyes of the Divine.

As we delve deeper into the nature of rivalry, we begin to recognize it as more than a simple clash of personalities. It is often rooted in a scarcity mentality, where one person's gain is believed to equate to another's loss. This toxic belief pervades relationships, both biblical and contemporary, suggesting that one's worth is diminished in the face of another's success. Peninnah's position as a mother did not grant her immunity from insecurity, while Hannah's barrenness became a symbol of her worthlessness in a world fixated on fertility. To understand this rivalry fully, we must also consider societal expectations during their time. The cultural narrative surrounding women often treated them as extensions of their husbands or children, leaving little room for individual identity or expression. Peninnah engaged in a vicious cycle of placing her worth in her ability to procreate, fueling her envy of Hannah and creating a toxic environment of competition. Hannah's silence is not merely a personal choice but a manifestation of societal pressures placed on women, where their identities become entangled with their perceived successes or failures in relational roles.

In contrasting Hannah and Peninnah, we must also acknowledge that rivalry often obscures one's ability to see the humanity of the other. Despite her actions, Peninnah is a mother, and her own journey toward self-acceptance is fraught with challenges. This complexity invites readers to consider the hearts of those we may view as rivals. Rather than reducing Peninnah to the role of a mere antagonist, we can explore the motivations behind her actions and the pain they reveal.

As Hannah's story unfolds, her relentless prayers highlight her desire for something beyond what Peninnah has, the blessing of motherhood, yes, but also the affirmation of her worth. This quest for identity is central to all women's lives. Hannah dares to hope and wrestle with God in her sorrow, demonstrating that vulnerability can lead to unearthly strength. When stripped of all societal definitions of success, Hannah's indomitable spirit shines through her despair, challenging modern readers to evaluate their own responses to rivalries in their lives.

Through the lens of Hannah's experiences, we are invited to reassess the rivalries we encounter in our own relationships. Often, these rivalries spring from unspoken fears and insecurities. When faced with conflict, it can be tempting to view the other woman not as a person with her own struggles but simply as an obstacle to overcome. This narrative can lead to isolation and heartbreak, where women find themselves in a cycle of competition rather than mutual support and understanding.

Moreover, Hannah's relationship with God serves as an anchor amid the turbulence of rivalry. She pours out her heart in prayer, which invites deeper reflection for anyone facing similar struggles. In her cries for help, she finds solace and a sense of identity apart from Peninnah's taunts. For women today, this offers the reminder that connecting with the Divine can help illuminate our self-worth beyond societal accolades or comparisons with others.

Rivalry can also become a catalyst for personal growth, revealing unresolved feelings and encouraging us to pursue healing. While Peninnah's actions illuminate the emotional scars of her own insecurities, they also set the stage for Hannah's transformation. As she emerges from her struggles, she inspires those who read her story to reconsider their approaches to conflict, potentially paving the way for empathy and understanding rather than hostility.

Reflecting on these themes, the narrative of Hannah and Peninnah invites deeper contemplation about our relationships in the modern world. How often do we find ourselves in positions of rivalry? In a world where comparison reigns supreme, especially in an age saturated with social media, it can sometimes be challenging to elevate each other's stories and journeys. We may find ourselves instinctively competing, allowing envy to seep into our relationships and cloud our judgments.

In dismantling the notion of rivalry, we recognize the beauty in shared experiences and wisdom gained from one another. Hannah's eventual triumph, birthed from her deep faith and relentless prayers, becomes more than a victory over Peninnah; it becomes a tribute to the strength of women facing adversity together. Hannah's ultimate gift, a son, Samuel, was not just a personal triumph; it became a blessing for the entire nation.

As we draw parallels between Hannah and women today, we realize that rivalry, while often painful, can also be constructive. Much like Peninnah, we may grapple with feelings of inadequacy that lead us to adopt a stance of competition and contention. Yet, Hannah's story serves as a reminder that we need not remain consumed by rivalry, but instead strive for authentic connections through support and encouragement. Each woman reflects God's image, and there is no need for competition over the gifts He bestows.

Even as Hannah's plight unfolds against the backdrop of rivalry, it is her journey of hope and faith that ultimately transcends her conflict. As her prayers rise to God, they become the groundwork for her transformation, enabling readers to seek their own moments of encounter with the Divine. Hannah's story encourages us not only to examine the lives of those who challenge us but to view these rivalries as vehicles for understanding and growth.

In navigating the complexities of rivalry, we are called to embrace vulnerability and honesty, allowing ourselves to confront our insecurities and the rivals we face. Whether in the chapters of our lives or the pages of scripture, we are reminded that our struggles can provide profound lessons on endurance, resilience, and ultimately, the power of faith. Just as the story of Hannah and Peninnah reflects the conflicts inherent in relationships, it also illuminates the path toward unity within the broader tapestry of womanhood.

In the end, the rivalry between Peninnah and Hannah offers us rich soil for introspection. It dares us to transform our rivalries into opportunities for connection, understanding, and mutual growth. As we strive to uplift one another in solidarity rather than compete for approval or recognition, we create a space where our differences can flourish into shared stories of grace and empowerment. Through the lens of Hannah's experience, we grasp a truth that withstands time: overcoming rivalry begins with acknowledging the intrinsic value of every woman's story, including our own. The journey of faith lies not just in seeking our own blessings but in fostering an environment where everyone can thrive.

Finding Resilience in Adversity

In the tapestry of life's challenges, few experiences are as poignant as the trials we face in relationships, especially those marked by rivalry and resentment. For Hannah, the second wife of Elkanah, her adversary Peninnah became a constant source of pain and humiliation. Peninnah's mockery surrounding Hannah's inability to conceive a child struck at the very core of Hannah's identity and self-worth. Yet, through the bitterness of their rivalry, Hannah embarked on an internal journey that would lead her toward profound resilience, one that was built not just in response to her circumstances but as a testament to her inner strength.

Hannah's story is intricately woven with the themes of adversity and the personal growth that can emerge from hardship. The challenge presented by Peninnah forced Hannah to confront deep-seated insecurities about her worth as a woman and her role in her family. In a culture where a woman's value was often measured by her ability to bear children, Hannah's pain was not merely emotional; it was societal. The scorn from Peninnah magnified her own fears and feelings of inadequacy, pushing her to the brink of despair. Yet, it is from this very despair that Hannah began to cultivate resilience.

Resilience is often defined as the capacity to recover quickly from difficulties, but it encompasses so much more. It involves a process of adjustment, transformation, and growth. For Hannah, the painful taunts of Peninnah became a catalyst for self-reflection. Amidst the anguish, Hannah sought not just to endure but to rise above her circumstances. This journey inward was perhaps her most significant battle. Instead of allowing herself to be defined by Peninnah's cruelty, Hannah turned her gaze toward herself and her relationship with God.

The act of turning inward during times of external strife is a powerful tool for resilience. Hannah began to pray fervently, pouring out her heart to God in the temple at Shiloh. In her prayers, Hannah found a safe space to wrestle with her emotions and lay bare her soul.

The bitterness she felt in response to Peninnah's rivalries became the impetus for an honest dialogue with God, who became her refuge. By directing her pain toward prayer rather than toward retaliation or self-pity, Hannah began to reclaim her agency in the narrative of her life.

In her prayers, Hannah expressed her deep desires and her heartache, the very things that Peninnah sought to exploit. The act of speaking her truth before God was transformative. It allowed Hannah to shift her focus from the judgments of others to a divine understanding of her worth. Despite the taunts and mockery, she began to realize that her value did not reside in her ability to conceive but in her faithfulness and her relationship with God. This epiphany became a vital cornerstone of her resilience.

As Hannah poured out her heart in prayer, she not only sought the blessing of motherhood but also understanding, strength, and peace. The resilience she built was rooted in a profound sense of hope. Hope is often the light that guides us through our darkest hours. For Hannah, the hope of being heard and answered by God strengthened her resolve. The bitterness that had threatened to consume her began to blossom into something beautiful – an unshakeable faith in God's plan.

We see the importance of community in cultivating resilience as well. Hannah was not alone in her struggle. She had Elkanah, her husband, who loved her deeply and offered her comfort. While it is easy to overlook the support from those around us in our darkest times, Hannah demonstrates the significance of recognizing and embracing this support as a means of fostering resilience. Elkanah's love provided Hannah with a foundation from which she could explore the depths of her pain without being alone. He reminded her of her worth, assuring her that she was more to him than just the sum of her fertility.

However, even the love of a husband cannot shield one from the sting of rivalry. Peninnah represented a side of life that couldn't be eradicated or ignored. Every mocking word she uttered served as a reminder of Hannah's perceived shortcomings. Yet, the same rivalry that humiliated Hannah inadvertently propelled her toward introspection and growth. It called forth a deeper understanding of herself and her relationship with God. In this paradox, Hannah found strength and resilience.

The resilience Hannah cultivated is a reflection of her unwavering faith and her ultimate trust in God's plan. Her journey reminds us that true strength arises not from a life devoid of challenges but through confronting adversity with grace. Hannah's decision to take her pain to God exemplifies the power of prayer as a means of finding inner strength. In the face of Peninnah's cruelty, Hannah transformed her suffering into an opportunity for spiritual growth and development. Ultimately, Hannah's story is one of triumph amid adversity. Her resilience did not lead her to conquer Peninnah or to seek revenge; rather, it positioned her to rise above the hurt and to become a figure of faith who would eventually give birth to Samuel, a significant prophet in Israel's history. In this way, her internal journey demonstrates that personal growth can arise out of even the most bitter rivalries and painful experiences.

To cultivate resilience in the face of adversity, it's essential to acknowledge the emotions that arise. Emotional honesty allows us to feel and process the pain rather than suppress it. Hannah exemplifies this when she pours out her soul before God, unreservedly expressing her anguish. Acknowledging the reality of our pain is the first step toward healing and growth. When we permit ourselves to be vulnerable, we open the door to resilience.

Moreover, leaning into our support systems is crucial. While Hannah's journey was deeply personal, her relationship with Elkanah, and ultimately, her relationship with God, served as vital anchors in turbulent times. Resilience flourishes in environments of love, acceptance, and encouragement. We must not shy away from seeking and embracing help from those who care for us as we navigate our own challenges. Furthermore, embracing hope is a pivotal aspect of resilience. Hannah clung to the hope that her situation would change, a hope sustained by her faith in God. In times of adversity, hope serves as a beacon; it fuels perseverance and assures us that our struggles can lead to something beautiful, even when the outcome is uncertain. As we face our Peninnahs, we must cultivate a hopeful spirit, trusting that, in due time, the fruit of our perseverance will be evident.

Finally, resilience requires patience. Just as Hannah's journey did not yield immediate results, neither do our struggles often resolve overnight. Perseverance in the face of adversity involves a commitment to endure and wait. Hannah's faithful prayers were a testament to her patience, and her eventual answer from God reminds us that waiting can be an integral part of the process. In our challenges, we are called to trust the timing of our lives, even when the wait feels unbearable.

Hannah's story is one of remarkable strength and growth born from the trials of a bitter rivalry. It serves as an inspiration for all women facing challenges, encouraging them to rise above the adversity that life throws their way. The lessons drawn from her experiences with Peninnah are poignant reminders that, through prayer, hope, and a commitment to self-reflection, we can become resilient in the face of any adversity. In discovering our strength amid strife, we mirror Hannah's journey toward personal growth, demonstrating that, like her, we too can flourish, ultimately finding our purpose beyond the pain. As we reflect upon Hannah's life, let us embrace the understanding that rivalries and challenges are not simply obstacles; they are opportunities for growth. By allowing them to shape us into more resilient individuals, we can harness the power of our experiences to uplift ourselves and others. Like Hannah, we can turn bitterness into personal transformation, emerging from our adversities stronger and more faithful than before. In this way, we invite the possibility of beginnings anew, where resilience blooms amidst the thorns of rivalry, leading us to a life of purpose and hope.

Lessons from Rivalry

In the quiet solitude of her heart, Hannah carried the weight of her dreams, a longing for a child that filled her thoughts and shaped her desires. Her womb was empty, but her spirit brimmed with hope. Yet, alongside her aspirations, she faced a relentless challenge in the form of Peninnah, her husband's other wife. Where Hannah's longing remained unfulfilled, Peninnah's fertility was a constant reminder of Hannah's perceived inadequacies. This rivalry, born out of stark contrasts in their circumstances, evolved into a profound journey of self-discovery for Hannah, revealing lessons that extended far beyond the confines of their shared home.

Rivalry can often be viewed through a negative lens, conjuring images of bitterness, jealousy, and pain. However, if we choose to reframe such conflicts, we can discover that they offer invaluable insights into our own depths and can ultimately drive us toward growth. Hannah's relationship with Peninnah is a testament to this. Instead of succumbing to desolation in the face of relentless competition, Hannah learns to channel her emotions, pushing her toward self-reflection and spiritual strength.

Initially, Hannah's experience with Peninnah was one of anguish. Every taunt and reminder of her own barrenness felt like a deep stab into her spirit. Peninnah's children signified not just her own fertility but also Hannah's perceived shortcomings as a woman and a wife. The years of silent longing became compounded by the public nature of Peninnah's motherhood. It was easy for Hannah to spiral into despair, to view her rival as a relentless force of negativity that overshadowed her existence. Yet, after enduring a cycle of pain, Hannah began to recognize that her feelings of inferiority were only feeding Peninnah's desire to dominate her emotionally.

Through the turbulence of emotional rivalry, Hannah's path toward self-discovery began. She learned that rivalry could be a mirror reflecting her deepest insecurities. Each encounter with Peninnah, each painful reminder of their contrasting fortunes, prompted

Hannah to look inward, forcing her to confront her feelings of worth and identity beyond motherhood. Rather than crisis, these moments became catalysts for transformation.

Hannah's emotional journey took shape during her visits to the temple, a sacred space that offered solace to her tumultuous spirit. While at the temple, she poured out her anguish to God. In her candor, she established a connection that transcended her rivalry with Peninnah. Here, the competitive landscape transformed into a sacred dialogue focused on her desires and dreams. Hannah's prayers became the intimate space where she started to believe in her intrinsic worth, independent of her status as a mother or Peninnah's perceptions. What began as despair evolved into a divine conversation, cultivating resilience.

The act of prayer also revealed another critical lesson for Hannah: the importance of vulnerability. In embracing her pain, she uncovered a strength that defied her own expectations. Vulnerability often feels like a weakness, especially when faced with rivalry, but Hannah discovered that it could be the very foundation for profound strength. By allowing herself to feel deeply, not just the bitterness of rivalry, but also the hopes and dreams that remained kindling in her heart, Hannah harnessed her true power. She gained clarity about what she truly wanted: not merely to have a child, but to build a deep and unshakeable connection with the Divine.

As Hannah's understanding of herself blossomed, her perspective on Peninnah began to shift. No longer solely a rival, Peninnah transformed into a complex figure representing a challenge, a challenge that became crucial for Hannah's growth. Instead of viewing her through the lens of jealousy, Hannah started to understand Peninnah as a part of the larger tapestry of her life. This shift in perception allowed room for compassion. Hannah recognized that Peninnah's actions, though hurtful, were often rooted in her own insecurities and societal pressures. Such realizations did not erase the pain but opened the door to empathy, a healing balm that softened the bitterness of rivalry.

With time, Hannah transitioned from a posture of resistance to one of acceptance. Dictionary definitions of rivalry indicate a sense of competition marked by hostility, yet rivalry can nurture a deep understanding of one's self. Encouraged by her evolving self-awareness, Hannah began using her encounters with Peninnah as lessons, moments through which she learned about endurance, patience, and the intricacies of relationship dynamics. Instead of viewing Peninnah's presence as a threat, she could see her as a teacher in disguise, presenting invaluable lessons about the complexities of womanhood, motherhood, and the ways different paths can entwine and diverge.

The story of Hannah and Peninnah is emblematic of the tensions women often face, not just in ancient times but in contemporary life as well. Women frequently find themselves in situations of rivalry, whether these arise from differing roles in family dynamics, professional ambitions, or societal expectations. Each rivalry presents a choice: to succumb to enmity or to rise above it, transforming it into an opportunity for growth. Hannah's struggle reminds us that the very presence of competition can often lead to self-discovery when approached with the right mindset.

Forging this transition does not come easily. Just as Hannah experienced moments of despair and betrayal, we too confront the raw emotions that accompany rivalry. The challenges brought forth by competition can often feel insurmountable, tainting our relationships and muddying our perceptions of self-worth. Yet, within these very hardships lies the potential for insight; it's a chance to uncover layers of our identity that perhaps have been overlooked in the monotony of life's struggles.

Through her journey with Peninnah, Hannah ultimately found the courage to develop a vision beyond her rivalry. By embracing her experiences as catalysts for personal growth and utilizing her vulnerabilities as pillars of strength, she blossomed into a remarkable woman. Each tear shed and each prayer uttered laid the foundation for the woman who would eventually be sought by God, not just to achieve motherhood, but as a model of unwavering faith and resilience.

In reflecting on Hannah's experiences, I realize that my own moments of rivalry have similarly shaped me. There were instances in my youth when competition felt all-consuming, particularly with peers who seemed to effortlessly excel in areas where I struggled. Instead of evolving into bitterness, I came to understand that these rivalries could illuminate the paths I needed to take to discover my unique strengths. Each competitive encounter became an opportunity to redefine my self-worth: how I perceived myself in relation to my peers became a canvas upon which I could paint my own narrative of success.

Just like Hannah, I learned to draw from my vulnerable moments. It was in acknowledging my insecurities and fears that I started to embolden the parts of myself that initially felt overshadowed. The moments I felt the most challenged by others became the moments I honored my own journey, applying lessons learned and pushing through moments of growth that were often cloaked in discomfort. Understanding that rivalry does not solely equate to hostility can change the way we interact with others. Instead of simply opposing one another in competition, we can view each other as co-travelers on the path of growth. It allows for rich conversations that foster understanding, breaking down the barriers that rivalry has erected. When we embrace the idea that competing isn't just about being better than someone else, but also about recognizing shared struggles, we open a doorway toward camaraderie and mutual support.

Ultimately, the lessons from Hannah's rivalry with Peninnah hold profound relevance in our lives today. When faced with competition, we can choose to reflect rather than react. By turning inward and seeking understanding in the face of rivalry, we invite opportunities for personal growth that illuminate our journey. In embracing challenges with resilience and vulnerability, we too can blossom in extraordinary ways, finding strength in heartfelt connections with ourselves and with others, just as Hannah did during her trials in the shadow of Peninnah.

Hannah's story is not merely a tale of rivalry; it's an inspiring narrative about self-discovery. Through her struggle, we learn that competition can serve as a guiding force in uncovering our truths, encouraging us to dig deep and emerge stronger, more profound, and more evolved. In the tapestry of life, the threads woven through rivalry can lead us to powerful transformations, teaching us to embrace challenges as opportunities for growth and connection. Embracing such lessons in our own narratives may be the key to finding understanding, compassion, and ultimately the inner strength necessary to flourish in the face of any rivalry that comes our way.

SAMUEL'S BIRTH:
THE MIRACLE OF FULFILLMENT

The Anticipation of a Miracle

Hannah stood at the entrance of the tabernacle, her heart a tempest of longing and faith. As she gazed upon the sacred space, memories flooded her mind, each painful heartbeat echoing her prayers offered in desperation and hope. For years, she had battled the silent storm of infertility, enduring the taunts of Peninnah, her husband Elkanah's other wife. But now, she had reached a new level of determination; she was no longer merely yearning for a child. She was waiting for a miracle.

The anticipation of a miracle is unlike any other feeling. It is a mingling of faith and yearning, a promise embraced with the entirety of one's being. Hannah's journey to this moment had been incredibly arduous, a passage filled with sorrow that only amplified her hope. Each visit to Shiloh created a tension between despair and the flicker of hope that what she longed for might still come to pass. It was the heart-wrenching contradiction of human experience: waiting faithfully while grappling with deep emotional wounds.

The pillars of the tabernacle, tall and watchful, seemed to reflect the weight of her years. Hannah knew the stories of women who prayed for children, women whose circumstances mirrored her own. Sarah, who bore Isaac in her old age; Rachel, who grieved for what she did not have. These narratives echoed around her, creating a tapestry of shared heartache and divine intervention. They were a reminder that God had written hope into the fabric of their lives, and as she stood there, she clung to the belief that her own story would intersect with the miraculous threads of these women.

Every prayer she uttered was steeped in urgency, laced with the rawness of her spirit. "O Lord of hosts, if You will indeed look on the affliction of Your maidservant and remember me…" These words became her lifeline, a lifeline tangled with desperation, yet fortified by unwavering faith. Hannah's anguish cried out to the heavens with an intensity that resonated deep within her, awakening a part of her spirit that refused to be silenced. She envisioned the child she longed for, a boy who would become a man, a leader, a prophet whose very name would proclaim her story to generations to come.

In the solitude of her prayers, Hannah envisioned waiting rooms of divine timing. They were heavy with the potential of arrival but devoid of certainty. Just as a seed buried beneath the earth cannot know the warmth of the sun until the right moment, Hannah understood that her prayers were more than a plea. They were an embrace of faith in God's timing. Each prayer added a layer to her anticipation, stretching her heart, molding it into a vessel of expectation.

The teachings of her ancestors echoed in her mind, guiding her through the arduous wait. Patience is not merely the passage of time; it is cultivating a garden of trust in the unseen, as in the life of Job, where the journey through suffering birthed resilience and faith, Hannah's waiting bore the same fruit. With every meal shared at the table, amidst the laughter and jabs from Peninnah, Hannah anchored herself in prayer. Every shared moment only further fueled her desire to seek divine intervention. She adorned her prayers with gratitude and fervor.

Hannah remembered her conversation with Elkanah. Funny how some conversations can hold the resonance of entire lifetimes. He had asked her why she wept and why she wouldn't eat, trying to comprehend the depth of her struggle. "Am I not better to you than ten sons?" he had questioned, the concern for her burden evident in his voice. But no amount of love could fill the chasm that her desires carved within her heart. It was paradoxical how joy could exist alongside despair. In her case, her husband's kindness remained a soothing balm to her spirit, while the desire for a child loomed large, ever-persistent.

As the sun set on another day without the news she longed to hear, Hannah felt the stirrings of sadness giving way to renewed fervor. She found solace in the sacred space of Shiloh. With each passing year, her soul grew more entwined with the concept of hope. She understood one powerful truth: the journey of anticipation can often be as profound as the miracle itself.

It was during one of these annual pilgrimages that she made a sacred vow so profound that it transcended her own desire. With her heart laid bare, she promised God, "If You will give me a son, then I will give him to the Lord all the days of his life, and no razor shall come upon his head." This promise was not only a plea but a commitment, infusing her anticipation with purpose. Her dream transformed from a desire for personal fulfillment to a deep longing to see that child serve the Lord and impact the world in ways she could not yet fathom.

Hannah's prayer became a storm of intimate conversations with God, a rhythm of silence woven with whispers of faith. Though surrounded by the sounds of worship, her spirit often fell into a silence that felt deafening. The act of surrender, not just of her dreams but of herself, served to deepen her relationship with God. She was learning that there was beauty in incompleteness, richness in the waiting, and power in surrender.

Yet, even amidst her faith, doubts occasionally crept in, knocking on the door of her resolve. She felt vulnerable as she watched others celebrate their own blessings, their miracles. Jealousy threatened to drown her spirit, whispering lies about being overlooked and unworthy of God's attention. But she fought back. Each negative thought, like a storm passing through her heart, made her anchor herself firmer in prayer. In moments of doubt, she thought of Job once more, his faith prevailing against all odds. Hannah realized that anticipation is often wrapped in the fabric of vulnerability.

One fateful day, while in prayer, tears streamed down her cheeks, blurring her vision. In that intimate moment, she felt the heavy weight of surrender wash over her spirit. "Lord, if You see fit to bless me with a son, I will gladly give him back to You." It was a vow that danced between longing and surrender, each word fanning the flame of hope still flickering within her.

In the backdrop of Hannah's anticipation lay the omnipresent understanding of God's providence. The realization that the timing of delivery lay firmly in His hands cultivated peace. It was in the waiting that Hannah's character was forged. The flames of longing shaped her into a woman of great strength, who would later pass that legacy on to her son, Samuel. As she poured over the psalms in her heart, she began to see herself in the stories of those who had gone before her, strong women defined not merely by their childlessness but by their undying faith.

As the season of harvest approached yet another year, Hannah felt her heart beating wildly with hope, but she also understood that anticipation is a double-edged sword. There was joy in waiting, yet the ache of longing often pierced deeper than she could admit. The dual nature of that experience, the pain intertwined with hope, became a tapestry of raw emotions stitched within her spirit. It was during these moments of prayer that she discovered the beauty of vulnerability, releasing the burdens of expectation into the loving hands of her Creator.

In the anticipation of a miracle, Hannah learned that transformation often accompanies waiting. She began to see that her deepest anguish had shifted into a profound understanding of God's faithfulness. Each passing year was not marked merely by the absence of a child, but rather by the cultivation of a relationship with the divine that had dramatically shaped her perspective. Her identity as a mother, a wife, and a woman was being woven intricately into the narrative of faith.

Hannah confronted the days that unfolded like open pages, waiting for something to change, knowing she was on a pilgrimage toward a promise. There were days filled with silent prayers and soft weeping, times of clinging to God despite the uncertainties that lingered like shadows. The anticipation itself became a kind of miracle, a powerful catalyst for change in her life and character.

Then came the moment of truth, an unexpected stirring within her spirit that hinted at the potential of answered prayers. As the seasons began to shift, hope blossomed anew, a whispering promise that something of great significance was about to emerge. Hannah felt alive in a way she had not felt before; anticipation ignited her spirit, and she found herself daring to believe that the long-awaited miracle was on the horizon. She began to embrace every moment as an opportunity, not just for herself, but as a future legacy she wished to create for her son.

Finally, one fateful day, amidst prayers woven thick with longing, Hannah felt a shift take place within her. That familiar yet elusive stirring transformed into a radiant promise, a flicker of new life. In that moment, the world around her seemed to fall silent; her spirit leaped in recognition that she was pregnant. The miracle she had waited for was manifesting, and the culmination of years spent on her knees had borne the fruit of joy she had long desired.

The journey she had undertaken had become one of understanding; it revealed how entwined anticipation is with faith. It was in that profound moment that Hannah comprehended the true weight of her vow, a gift that she would eventually offer back to the Lord. Samuel's birth was not just a celebration of motherhood; it was the fulfillment of a promise steeped in divine timing and profound grace.

In the days that followed the miraculous announcement, Hannah exuded a greater sense of faith; she had become a vessel carrying not just a child but a legacy of worship. Her prayers had been heard, her anticipation had yielded a miracle, and she was ready to fulfill her vow to God. Samuel's arrival was not merely the end of her longing but the beginning of a new journey, one where she would raise him in a spirit of gratitude and a commitment to serving the Lord.

Hannah's story, intricately woven with strands of anticipation, divine timing, and the joy of answered prayers, serves as a powerful reminder of how God honors our desires while simultaneously inviting us to surrender. Through longing, pain, and unwavering faith, she exemplified the beauty of waiting. It is a narrative that invites us all to embrace our own journeys, rejoicing in the anticipation of our miracles and recognizing that sometimes, the path to fulfillment is the very foundation upon which our faith is built.

Celebration of New Beginnings

The birth of Samuel stands as a monumental event not only in Hannah's life but also in the history of Israel. It marked the culmination of years of yearning, prayer, and unwavering faith. In the wake of his arrival, the air vibrated with joy, anticipation, and profound gratitude, a testament to the miracle that had unfolded. This period of celebration was not merely personal for Hannah; it was deeply intertwined with the cultural practices of her community, which amplified the weight of her miracle and offered a glimpse into the essence of new beginnings.

To understand the significance of Samuel's birth, we must first explore the societal norms and practices surrounding childbirth in ancient Israel. In a culture that heavily emphasized family lineage and heritage, the arrival of a child was often seen as a blessing from God, a mark of favor that affirmed a woman's status in her community. For women like Hannah, who had endured the stigma of barrenness, the birth of a child was not just a personal victory; it was a narrative of redemption.

In biblical times, childbirth was framed within a communal context. Friends, family, and neighbors would gather to support the mother during labor, reflecting a collective spirit intertwined with the sacredness of new life. Celebratory traditions began even before the baby's arrival. As Hannah neared the end of her pregnancy, it would have been customary for her to be surrounded by other women, who would offer their wisdom, support, and encouragement. These women understood the tensions of pregnancy: the anticipation, the fear, the hopes, and the dreams for the future. They shared in the communal excitement, their voices weaving a tapestry of prayers and blessings over Hannah as her time to deliver approached.

When Samuel finally arrived, the atmosphere erupted in celebration. The community's joy would have been palpable, echoing through the streets. Friends and extended family would come bearing gifts, meals, and blessings, eager to share in the delight of Hannah's miracle. A child was more than just a new addition to a family; he was the embodiment of hope, a promise of continuity, and a symbol of God's faithfulness. This reverence for childbirth underlined the understanding that every new life was intrinsically linked to divine providence.

Traditionally, the naming of the child was a significant event. Names were chosen carefully, as they often encapsulated a hope or a story. In naming her son Samuel, meaning "God has heard," Hannah was publicly declaring the miracle that God had performed in her life. It wasn't just an acknowledgment of her individual struggle; it was a proclamation of faith that resonated throughout her community. Amidst the celebrations, this act of naming became a testament to God's attentive ear to her pleas, a signal that the old chapter of her life, marked by longing and despair, had given way to a new narrative brimming with possibility.

The cultural practice of celebrating childbirth did not end with the initial announcement of a baby's birth. Following the event, a period of joyous festivities would ensue. Friends and family would gather for a feast, sharing stories and laughter in honor of the child. This celebration was not merely a banquet; it was a ritual imbued with deep significance, a communal acknowledgment of life and the divine hand at work. Food, as a means of bonding, played a crucial role in these gatherings, serving both to nourish and to symbolize abundance. It was not uncommon for families to hold a naming ceremony within days of birth, bringing together those who had prayed for the child's arrival, reinforcing ties and shared beliefs. In the case of Hannah, one can imagine the fervor of the celebration growing as news spread. The townsfolk, who had perhaps witnessed her struggles, would have felt a sense of collective joy. They had participated in her anguish through their own reflective prayers and had longed for her breakthrough. Now that Samuel had arrived, they rejoiced with her as if he were their own. In celebrating Samuel's birth, they were ultimately celebrating the faithfulness of God and inviting others to partake in the story of transformation that Hannah had experienced.

Emotional expressions during childbirth were also deeply rooted in the customs of the time. Women offered maternal blessings filled with encouragement and words of wisdom, often invoking spiritual significance. The birth of Samuel would have stirred new hopes in the hearts of those women gathered alongside Hannah. New beginnings spark dreams and aspirations, and the presence of a newborn usually reignites faith in the miraculous. Each woman in attendance likely carried her own burdens and ambitions, believing that a new life could usher in prosperity, not just for Hannah, but for the entire community.

As guests united in gratitude and celebrations, music and dance would fill the air, creating an atmosphere charged with exuberance. Symbolic of the joy of new beginnings, these expressions were a vital part of the festivities, highlighting an essential aspect of cultural practices surrounding childbirth. Within Hannah's community, songs of rejoicing accompanied the arrival of a child, verses celebrating God's goodness, the promises made, and the miraculous answers to prayers. The narrative of Samuel's birth would become a story passed on through the generations, underscoring the weight of expectation that accompanies new beginnings.

Moreover, childbirth rituals in this era often emphasized the transition of a woman's identity. For Hannah, becoming a mother transformed her from a woman marked by her barrenness into one defined by her fulfillment. This transition celebrated the innate value of womanhood and motherhood within ancient cultures. As Samuel entered the world, Hannah entered a territory of respect and reverence. The rituals surrounding childbirth served to elevate her status within her community, as motherhood was honored and revered. This ceremony of transformation was not solely limited to her own experience; it represented a significant shift for many women who had felt the crushing weight of shame and societal judgment.

Yet, underlying all the joy was the understanding that new beginnings can also birth challenges. Samuel's arrival came with expectations that both Hannah and her community embraced. The blessing of a child often catalyzed a heightened sense of responsibility. Alongside their reaped joy was the understanding that with miraculous blessings come divine responsibilities. Hannah was entrusted with Samuel's upbringing, a role that would require her to instill faith, values, and purpose. This dual layer of celebration and responsibility illustrates the complexities of new beginnings; every joyous occasion may also introduce new terrains of growth, challenge, and commitment.

In retrospect, every significant life event in the Bible, much like Hannah's experience surrounding Samuel's birth, illustrates the intricate interplay between the joy of fulfillment and the weight of responsibility. Hannah's journey serves as a reminder for women today that new beginnings, whether they pertain to motherhood, a new job, or any transformative life event, are celebrated not just for the joy they bring but also for the challenges they present.

As we consider the breadth of Hannah's story, each facet invites us to reflect on our own experiences of new beginnings. The essence of joy interwoven with responsibility transcends time, speaking to our inherent need for connection, affirmation, and community. Each new chapter in our lives can be a mirror reflecting the ancient customs that underscore our shared humanity. Hannah did more than celebrate a new life; she embraced an opportunity for growth that would span beyond her own story. Samuel, who would later emerge as a prophet and leader, was a vessel of change not only for his mother but for an entire nation. His birth was a profound reminder that a seemingly small miracle can possess the seeds of great transformation. Through this lens, we can appreciate the rich cultural tapestry surrounding the birth of Samuel, an event that was less about the singular joy of a mother and more about the birth of hope and promise within an entirety. In celebrating new beginnings, we engage in the profound truth that community, responsibility, and shared joy illuminate the narratives of our lives, echoing throughout time and forging connections that resonate with every generation. The weight of Hannah's miracle continues to inspire women everywhere, reminding us that every new birth, every beginning we celebrate, is a potent reminder of the extraordinary potential woven into the fabric of our lives.

Hannah's Dedication

Hannah's commitment to dedicate her son Samuel to God is one of the most poignant moments in the biblical narrative. It goes beyond the sorrow of her infertility; it encapsulates a profound act of faith that reverberates through generations. Her vow, born out of anguish, emerges as one of the key factors that transform not only her life but also the trajectory of Israel's spiritual and political landscape. Within the delicate balance of hope and despair, Hannah personifies the tension between personal desires and divine plans, a theme that resonates deeply with our contemporary struggles.

When Hannah found herself in the temple, beseeching the Lord for a child, she made a vow that would change everything. Her words display the raw intensity of her longing: "O Lord of hosts, if You will indeed look on the affliction of Your servant and remember me, and not forget Your servant, but will give to Your servant a son, then I will give him to the Lord all the days of his life." With this vow, Hannah encapsulates the essence of dedication, not merely an act of giving away, but an acknowledgment that true fulfillment becomes accessible through sacrifice.

The passion of her request signals a heart that is not only desperate but also deeply rooted in faith. This sacred moment raises questions about the nature of commitment. From the surface, it might seem that Hannah seeks to fulfill her personal desire for motherhood, yet she balances this yearning with a radical promise to dedicate her child wholly to God. In doing so, she challenges us to examine our own commitments. How often do we tether our hopes to God's plans, measuring our success against His purposes?

The notion of sacrifice is central to Hannah's dedication of Samuel. It requires immense humility to offer back to God what we desire most. Hannah's commitment does not come without a cost; she is not merely giving away a child, but she is surrendering her most profound dream. This act reflects the spiritual understanding that what we hold dear can also serve a higher purpose. Samuel was not just a son in her eyes; he was a gift from God that she recognized should be returned to the Giver, opening the door for divine intervention to reshape her own life and that of her community.

Hannah's narrative also emphasizes gratitude. After years of shame and social exclusion, the birth of Samuel catalyzed a radical transformation in her heart, prompting her to express gratitude through song. When she dedicates Samuel, she does not merely hand him over; she celebrates a fulfillment that is as much spiritual as it is physical. The hymn that follows Samuel's birth reveals the intimate relationship she has developed with God, a relationship marked by faith, recognition of God's sovereignty, and profound gratitude. This underscores an essential lesson: in our moments of receiving, we must also remember to express our gratitude, reflecting an understanding that our blessings often extend beyond personal gain to serve a broader purpose.

Through the act of dedicating Samuel, Hannah models the act of recognizing God's purpose in our own lives. This dedication speaks to the importance of aligning personal aspirations with divine intentions. She lays the groundwork for Samuel's future leadership, as her sacrifice nurtures the emergence of a prophet who would lead a nation. This interconnection of personal and communal destinies urges us to recognize that our commitments, whether to a child, a cause, or a faith, have implications that transcend our immediate desires. Each decision we make has the power to shape not just our own lives but the lives of those around us.

As readers engage with Hannah's dedication of Samuel, they are invited to explore the intricate relationships between sacrifice and purpose in their own lives. Does the act of dedicating something of great value resonate with their personal journeys? Hannah's story prompts introspection about how we respond to the calling God places on our hearts, encouraging us to consider what personal sacrifices we need to make in order to align ourselves with His will.

In a world where personal ambition often overshadows spiritual life, Hannah's unwavering faith offers a powerful counter-narrative. Her act of dedication serves as a clarion call to pursue not just what we want, but what aligns with God's greater plan. As we reflect on Hannah's vow and the subsequent dedication of Samuel, we are nudged towards a realm of freedom found in surrender. When we surrender our greatest hopes and dreams to God, we open ourselves to a reality where divine plans flourish, creating a tapestry of blessings that often exceed our understanding.

In contemplating Hannah's vow and her profound dedication to Samuel, it becomes clear that this moment invites a re-evaluation of our understanding of commitment. Obedience and sacrifice are woven into the fabric of faith, allowing us to experience the fullness of God's plans. Much like Hannah, we are called to offer our dreams and desires to the Lord, trusting that He will weave them into a beautiful narrative far beyond our personal expectations. The pathway to understanding our own commitment emerges through this lens, the reminder that sacrificial love leads to ultimate fulfillment, both individually and collectively.

Therefore, as we approach our own commitments, whether they be to family, community, or faith, Hannah's dedication to Samuel serves as a profound model. It beckons us to seek clarity in our desires, evaluate our aspirations, and ultimately align ourselves more closely with what God desires to accomplish through our lives. In doing so, we come to realize that dedicating ourselves means providing a canvas for God to paint His masterpiece, illustrating His divine purpose through our willingness to sacrifice and embrace His call. Through Hannah's story, we learn that fulfillment lies not just in receiving but in the beauty of giving, a testament to the power of commitment that shapes generations.

LESSONS FROM RUTH: LOYALTY UNDER THE DUSK

Ruth's Dedication to Naomi

Ruth's journey from Moab to Bethlehem is a powerful testament to loyalty and devotion, themes that resonate deeply within the tapestry of biblical narratives. At the heart of Ruth's story lies her unwavering commitment to her mother-in-law, Naomi, a relationship that transcends mere familial duty and blossoms into an expression of profound love. Ruth's decision to accompany Naomi back to her homeland marks the beginning of a transformative journey filled with challenges, heartbreak, and ultimately, redemption. This subchapter delves into the essence of Ruth's dedication to Naomi, drawing parallels to Hannah's resilience and portraying how both women faced extraordinary trials with extraordinary fortitude.

The backdrop of Ruth's loyalty begins with the narrative set during the time of the judges in Israel, a period marred by instability and uncertainty. After the death of her husband, Ruth is confronted with the daunting prospect of remaining in Moab, her homeland, or embarking on an uncertain journey with Naomi, who is also bereaved. The decision is fraught with complexity; staying in Moab means familiarity and cultural comfort, while following Naomi into an unknown land represents both sacrifice and commitment.

Ruth's declaration to Naomi is iconic: "Where you go, I will go, and where you stay, I will stay. Your people will be my people, and your God my God." This profound statement encapsulates not just loyalty but a deep-rooted selflessness, highlighting Ruth's willingness to abandon her past for the sake of her future with Naomi. It resonates with the essence of adhering to one's commitments, much like Hannah's unwavering devotion to her promise made to God. While Hannah's story reflects her longing for a child and her ultimate dedication of that child back to God, Ruth's narrative showcases a different aspect of commitment, one rooted in human relationships and familial bonds.

The juxtaposition of both women illuminates the theme of resilience against adversity. Hannah, despite her struggles with infertility and societal ridicule, remains steadfast in her faith, praying fervently for a son. Her loyalty to her promise, as she dedicates Samuel to the Lord, demonstrates a deep commitment to a higher calling. Similarly, Ruth's choice to leave everything familiar behind to support and care for Naomi reveals her strength in the face of societal expectations. As a Moabite, Ruth is an outsider in Bethlehem, yet she embraces the unknown, paralleling Hannah's journey of faith that leads her to trust in God's plan despite her trials.

Ruth's journey is not merely a physical relocation; it represents a spiritual transition as well. By choosing to follow Naomi and adopting her faith, Ruth enters a covenant community that is foreign to her. This act of loyalty is significant, as it signifies Ruth's integration into a new culture and belief system. Her commitment to Naomi transcends cultural boundaries, illustrating the power of love and loyalty over nationality or lineage. This mirrors Hannah's experience, who, as a woman in a patriarchal society, also navigates societal challenges through her faith and unwavering dedication.

However, the path Ruth chooses is fraught with difficulties. Upon arriving in Bethlehem, she faces the harsh realities of being a widow in a foreign land. The challenges of poverty and vulnerability loom large as she seeks to provide for Naomi and herself. The significance of Ruth gleaning in the fields can be seen as an act of both loyalty and hard work, symbolizing her dedication not only to Naomi but to survival itself. This practical manifestation of her commitment stands in stark contrast to the spiritual dedication exhibited by Hannah in her pursuit of motherhood. Ruth's resilience shines through her unwavering work ethic and determination. She doesn't shy away from hardship but embraces it as part of her new reality. The cultural norms of the time dictated a certain subservience for women, yet Ruth steps into the fields owned by Boaz with courage and dignity. Her identity begins to shift from that of a foreigner to one of respect and recognition, illustrating how loyalty and hard work can alter one's status within a community. This transformation also parallels the journey of Hannah. Her dedication to God is met with a profound blessing when she gives birth to Samuel. Through Hannah's obedience, she wins favor, and her life transforms as she becomes a mother. Likewise, Ruth's initial selflessness and hard work soon catch the attention of Boaz. His kindness and generosity become a pivotal moment in her life, a blessing that springs from her loyalty to Naomi and her unwavering resolve.

As Ruth continues to work in the fields, Naomi recognizes the favor that Ruth has found in Boaz. Encouraging Ruth to seek a relationship with him, Naomi steps into a role of guidance, demonstrating another layer of loyalty, this time, from Naomi towards Ruth. The bond between these two women evolves from one of dependence to mutual respect and empowerment, showcasing the depth of their relationship. Naomi's wisdom reflects her love, parallel to how Hannah's experiences teach her valuable lessons about faith, prayer, and dedication.

Ruth's loyalty is further highlighted in her courageous approach to Boaz. By uncovering his feet while he sleeps and lying down in a position of humility, Ruth is not just expressing her desire for him to act as a kinsman-redeemer; she is showcasing her faith in the unfolding of God's plan and her trust in Boaz's character. This act, while daunting for her, is marked by a deep sense of commitment, not only to her family's legacy but to Naomi's future as well. In both stories, we see how loyalty is tested in tumultuous times. Hannah's resolve to dedicate her son to God after years of anguish demonstrates her steadfast devotion, while Ruth's tenacity in remaining loyal to Naomi amidst societal challenges speaks to the same unwavering spirit. Both women emerge from their trials with newfound identities: Hannah as a blessed mother who fulfills her promise to God, and Ruth as a woman honored and respected in a new community, woven into the very fabric of Israel's history.

The marriage of Ruth and Boaz not only serves as the climax of her loyalty but also as a significant turning point in the narrative of Israel. Their union leads to the birth of Obed, who becomes the grandfather of King David. This lineage would eventually lead to the birth of Jesus, underscoring how loyalty and dedication, even in the face of adversity, can have far-reaching consequences. Ruth's faithfulness to Naomi and her willingness to embrace a new life marked the beginning of a legacy that extended beyond her immediate circumstances.

In studying Ruth's dedication to Naomi alongside Hannah's steadfastness, it becomes evident that loyalty is a powerful force that can shape destinies. Both women faced immense trials but held onto their commitments through thick and thin. Hannah's promise to God is echoed in Ruth's commitment to her mother-in-law, a loyalty that defies cultural norms and social expectations. Their stories remind us of the importance of selflessness and resilience, teaching us that even amidst trials, acts of love and loyalty can lead to redemption, blessing, and hope.

As we reflect on Ruth's remarkable journey and her unwavering dedication to Naomi, we are encouraged to examine our own lives. How do we express loyalty in our relationships? Are we willing to sacrifice for those we love, even when circumstances are challenging? Ruth's story pushes us to embrace our commitments, reminding us that loyalty is not always convenient, but it is often a path that leads to abundant blessings. Just as Hannah found fulfillment in her faith and dedication, we, too, can find purpose and strength when we embody the spirit of loyalty that both Ruth and Hannah exemplified.

The essence of Ruth's dedication to Naomi reveals a profound truth about the nature of love: it is selfless, courageous, and unwavering. It teaches us that true loyalty is not merely a response to obligation but a deep-rooted commitment to those we cherish. In a world where relationships often falter under pressure, the stories of these two remarkable women inspire us to dig deeper and uphold the bonds we hold dear, especially in times of adversity. Ruth and Hannah remind us that through loyalty, we not only honor those we love but also pave the way for future generations to experience the blessings that arise from a heart committed to selfless love.

The Symbolism of Gleaning

In the fields of ancient Israel, where the sun gilded the edges of each ear of grain, gleaning was not merely a means of survival but a rich practice woven with threads of hope, persistence, and ultimately, divine grace that sustains us all. The act of gleaning, as exemplified by Ruth, serves as a powerful metaphor for both physical sustenance and spiritual fulfillment, a dual purpose that resonates deeply within the narratives of women in the Scriptures, particularly in the life of Hannah. To glean is to gather what remains after the harvest, a practice rooted in the laws handed down to the Israelites, reflecting God's commitment to justice and compassion. In the book of Leviticus, we find the directive: "When you reap the harvest of your land, do not reap to the very edges of your field or gather the gleanings of your harvest. Leave them for the poor and the foreigner" (Leviticus 23:22). This act is emblematic of God's heart for the marginalized, a tangible commitment to ensure that those in need would find sustenance. Ruth embodies this principle, approaching the fields of Boaz with her heart set on survival not only for herself but also for her mother-in-law, Naomi.

Ruth's loyalty to Naomi opened her life to the rich experience of gleaning. By going out to the fields, she not only demonstrated her tenacity but also a profound understanding of support and sacrifice. Her willingness to glean serves as a poignant reminder of how our physical actions often reflect deeper spiritual truths. In Ruth's determination to provide for her family, we find echoes of Hannah's own story; both women navigate the thorny paths of sacrifice, and both display a relentless spirit that seeks sustenance not just for themselves but for those they love.

Gleaning, then, is about more than the physical act of collecting leftover grain; it symbolizes the spiritual provision we glean from our experiences. In many ways, Ruth's gleaning in Boaz's fields mirrors Hannah's sacrifice in the temple, where she poured out her soul in prayer, pleading for a child. Each woman, through her labor, whether in the fields or in the house of God, sought fulfillment and a legacy that would extend beyond her immediate life.

The spiritual underpinnings of gleaning extend to the essence of interconnectedness among generations. Ruth's gleaning efforts were not solely for her contemporaneous needs but were an act of faith that would ripple through time, ultimately leading to her place in the lineage of David, and by extension, of Jesus Christ. This natural succession invites readers to examine their own lives and the legacies they are building. Each act of love, sacrifice, and devotion becomes an opportunity to glean from the rich soil of our faith and heritage, nurturing connections that span across generations.

Examining the relationship between Hannah and Ruth reveals a continuum of faith and action. While Ruth physically gathered in the fields, Hannah metaphorically gathered strength from her relationship with God, her prayers serving as a yielding of her spirit, offering her very essence in the pursuit of motherhood. Much like Ruth, Hannah's gleaning was intense and sacrificial; her pleas were raised in an atmosphere of desperation, where the weight of her longing for a child bore down upon her heart.

In moments of vulnerability, when Hannah stood in the temple, her lips moving with the profound cry of her heart, she was, at that moment, gleaning from the very soil of faith. She harvested hope from the depths of her despair, believing that God would intervene. Hannah's act of laying herself bare before the Lord embodies the essence of gleaning, gathering spiritual sustenance from the very presence of God. Ruth, standing in the fields collecting barley, echoed this sentiment; each handful she collected was a testament to her faith, her loyalty to Naomi, and her understanding that sustenance requires effort and trust in God's provision.

The act of gleaning reminds us that spiritual sustenance sometimes comes in unexpected forms. Much like those remnants of grain left behind for the gleaners, God's blessings often appear in the most unlikely places. For Hannah, her journey to motherhood was fraught with sorrow and shame, tinged with a culture that valued women largely by their ability to bear children. Yet, in her deep anguish, she continued to glean from her faith, relying on the promise that God listens and sees our pain. This duality of mankind's struggle with outward appearances versus inward faith is crucial. Just as Ruth gleaned diligently in Boaz's fields, seeking sustenance for her family, Hannah's appeal to God for a child was a silent gleaning of faith. Both women teach us that the act of seeking, whether through tangible effort or desperate prayer, is met with divine acknowledgment.

Furthermore, gleaning in this context becomes an exercise in humility. It requires one to recognize their limitations and to rely on the sustenance found beyond oneself. Ruth clearly accepted her vulnerable position as a Moabitess gleaning in the fields of an Israelite, yet she moved forward with purpose. This speaks volumes to Hannah's narrative as well. There she was, in a place of anguish, pouring out her heart amidst the taunts of Peninnah, her rival. Both women faced societal pressures and personal insecurities but remained undeterred in their pursuits.

In this light, we see that gleaning is an act of service, as both women sought to serve those they loved. Ruth served Naomi by risking her own safety and status in a foreign land, tirelessly working for the welfare of her mother-in-law. Similarly, Hannah's sacrifice; offering her longed-for child to God, speaks of her willingness to serve God's purpose above her personal desires, illustrating that true fulfillment often comes through selfless acts. This call to serve others can transcend generations; the hard-earned lessons of love and loyalty bequeathed from one woman to another. In recounting these legacies, we must acknowledge that the act of gleaning is inherently communal. Ruth gleaned not only for herself but in solidarity with Naomi. Hannah's devotion ushered in the story of Samuel, who became a great prophet and leader, guiding Israel in their relationship with God. The sacrifices made by these women set in motion a divine plan that reached far beyond their immediate circumstances, inspiring generations to come.

Reflecting on the impact of Ruth and Hannah, we realize that their journeys teach us how to glean wisdom from our own hardships and the trials experienced by the women before us. Their narratives become an inheritance from which we can draw strength and insight. In sharing our stories of resilience and faith, we invite future generations to glean from our experiences, offering them both hope and encouragement.

As we consider the symbolism of gleaning, let us engage in the practice of looking beyond the immediate circumstances and harvesting deeper truths. Each woman's story serves as an invitation to reflect on what we glean from the fields of our own lives. How do we embrace our vulnerabilities, nurture our relationships, and extract wisdom from the remnants of our trials? In modern contexts, our fields may not be literal. Yet, the act of gleaning is ever-present in the spiritual and emotional labor we undertake as we navigate today's complexities. It's the gathering of insights from our communities, from mentors who share their wisdom, and from the lessons learned in the aftermath of our struggles. Like Ruth and Hannah, we are called to persevere, to seek out sustenance in our relationships, and to act with loyalty and love, ensuring that the legacies we leave behind become sources of nourishment for those who follow.

In closing, the symbolism of gleaning within the narratives of Ruth and Hannah encapsulates a wealth of life lessons, lessons that thrive in the intersection of loyalty, sacrifice, and the pursuit of spiritual fulfillment. Their stories remind us that while we may glean from the edges of fields, it is the heart with which we seek that ultimately enriches our lives and shapes our legacies. Gleaning, then, becomes a celebration of the unseen, an embrace of the sacred commitment to family, and an acknowledgment of the divine sustenance that flows through our connections and our faith. Weaving these lessons into our lives, we honor the stories of those who have gone before us and lay down a path for those who will glean from our journey in the years to come.

Transformation Through Relationships

In the unfolding stories of the women in the Bible, we find remarkable illustrations of the transformative power of relationships. In particular, the tales of Hannah and Ruth present us with profound lessons on loyalty, connection, and personal growth through the bonds we forge with others. At first glance, their narratives may seem distinct, each navigating a different set of challenges and emotions. However, upon closer examination, it becomes evident that a common thread tethers both women: the impact of their relationships on their personal development and resilience in the face of adversity.

Hannah, often cloaked in sorrow and longing, represents the heart of a mother. Her fervent prayers at the temple, fueled by her deep desire for a child, speak volumes about the connection she has with God and the desperation she feels in the wake of her barrenness. Her relationship with her husband, Elkanah, though filled with love, is shadowed by the presence of Peninnah, his other wife, who taunts her openly. Yet, within this tumultuous environment, Hannah's strength begins to reveal itself, growing in part because of these relationships.

Ruth, on the other hand, emerges from a backdrop of loss and loyalty. Her bond with Naomi, her mother-in-law, becomes the source of her transformation. After losing her husband, Ruth could have returned to her homeland of Moab to start anew, but her dedication to Naomi, who had lost everything, defines her character. Ruth's relationship with Naomi fuels her resilience and ambition, ultimately leading her to Bethlehem, where she chooses a life filled with challenges but ripe with possibility. These intertwining stories of Hannah and Ruth illuminate how love and loyalty can foster personal growth, encouraging readers to reflect on the relationships in their own lives.

Examining the bond between Hannah and God reveals an essential aspect of transformation through relationships. Hannah's desperation for a child is not merely a personal longing; it encapsulates her desire to be a part of a lineage, a community, and a divine plan. In her darkest moments, she ventures into the temple to pray with a spirit of anguish, pouring her heart out and seeking refuge in her relationship with God. This act of vulnerability symbolizes her plea for connection, not only with her husband but also with a higher calling. God's eventual response to her prayers serves as a testament to how her relationship with Him fosters transformation. Hannah's experience encourages the understanding that our spiritual relationships can bear fruit in the most profound ways, often encouraging us to embrace our own authenticity and resilience.

Furthermore, Hannah's relationship with Elkanah plays a crucial role in her transformation. Elkanah's love and support demonstrate the importance of a partner who recognizes both our pain and potential. He reassures Hannah that her worth is not solely tethered to motherhood but resides in her value as a person. His gentle encouragement bolsters her resolve, allowing her to wrestle with God without fear of judgment or abandonment. Elkanah's investments in her emotional well-being serve as a reminder that relationships can empower us to seek our desires with fervor, to endure hardships with strength, and to find solace in love amidst pain.

Ruth's relationship with Naomi, in another light, depicts the essence of loyalty and its transformative power. It is her commitment to Naomi despite the loss that highlights the profound nature of their bond. When Ruth declares, "Where you go, I will go; where you stay, I will stay," she expresses not only a promise of physical companionship but also an emotional covenant of support and loyalty. This vow becomes the bedrock of Ruth's identity, a legacy of love that transcends cultural boundaries and societal expectations. It elevates her from a widow of Moab to a significant figure in the lineage of David and ultimately of Christ.

Through loyalty, Ruth exemplifies how relationships can shape our destinies. She does not simply follow Naomi to Bethlehem; she embraces the uncertainty that accompanies it. Ruth's acceptance of both the challenges and joys of leaving her homeland illustrates profound bravery grounded in love and loyalty. In the face of adversity, she embodies the remarkable resilience that occurs when we have strong relationships that support our journey, as they propel us into unfamiliar territory that may lead to growth and transformation.

The bond between Ruth and Naomi also adds another layer to our understanding of relationships and transformation. Naomi, devastated by loss, initially tries to dissuade Ruth from accompanying her. In decline, Naomi embodies grief, feeling isolated and vulnerable in a land foreign to her. Yet, Ruth's loyalty acts as a lifeline, pulling Naomi from despair. Their complex relationship is not simply one-sided; it evolves as they navigate their struggles together. Naomi's eventual acceptance of Ruth's determination fosters a partnership that allows both of them to flourish in their own unique ways. Through shared grief, love thrives, showcasing how relationships can be the crucible for personal growth and mutual support.

In reflecting on their stories, it is crucial to evaluate our own relationships, who we choose to stand by, who supports us in our hardest times, and to what extent we allow ourselves to lean into these connections. Hannah's willingness to be vulnerable with God and Elkanah, and Ruth's fierce loyalty to Naomi, illustrate pathways toward transformation grounded in heartfelt relationships. These narratives prompt introspection: Are we fostering connections that uplift us? Are we nurturing bonds that encourage us to grow? Are we, in turn, providing the same support to others?

Moreover, it's essential to recognize that relationships can take many shapes. They can be rooted in familial ties, friendships, mentorships, or spiritual connections. Each holds the potential to foster transformation. In an era characterized by transient and sometimes superficial relationships, these stories remind us of the immeasurable strength found within steadfast loyalty and love. The relationships that we cultivate, whether with family, friends, or within our community, hold the transformative potential to shape us, often in unexpected ways. As believers, we are called to embrace relationships infused with compassion and empathy. Hannah and Ruth shine as models of how love can push us beyond our perceived limitations and challenge us to move forward, even when the path before us is unclear. For readers, the lesson is unmistakable: growth often occurs not in isolation, but in communion with others who walk alongside us. Intentional relationships grounded in love, loyalty, and mutual support provide a nurturing environment where transformation can unfold.

In conclusion, the stories of Hannah and Ruth remind us that relationships are central to our journeys. They have the power to uplift, to challenge, and ultimately, to transform us. As we navigate our own lives, let us cultivate connections that resonate with the depth of loyalty seen in these biblical figures. Let us embrace the transformative journeys that occur when we invest in relationships, those that raise our spirits, broaden our horizons, and lead us closer to our true selves. Equipped with these insights, we can walk forward into our futures, forging paths of resilience and empowerment grounded in the bonds of love and loyalty we choose to nurture. Just as Hannah and Ruth exemplified, our relationships are not just threads in our narratives; they are the very fabric of our stories, weaving together our destinies in ways we may not yet fully comprehend.

DEBORAH'S STRENGTH: A BEACON OF LEADERSHIP

Understanding Deborah's Context

In the sweep of biblical history, the role of women has often been underexplored, overshadowed by their male counterparts. However, the life and leadership of Deborah stand as a testament to the strength and resilience women brought to the community of faith and governance in ancient Israel. To understand Deborah's unique position as a prophetess and a judge, it is essential to delve into the historical context of her time, including the socio-political climate, cultural beliefs, and the dynamics of faith that characterized the Age of the Judges.

The period of the Judges, set between the conquest of Canaan under Joshua and the establishment of monarchy in Israel, was marked by tumultuous circumstances. Israel lacked a central governing authority and was instead led by a series of judges who rose to prominence during times of national crisis. The cyclical pattern of sin, oppression, repentance, and deliverance defined this era, with the Israelites frequently turning away from God and facing the consequences. Deborah's leadership did not emerge in a vacuum; rather, it arose from the collective struggles and aspirations of her people as they grappled with identity, loyalty, and the divine call in the face of longstanding adversaries.

Deborah, whose name means "bee," signifies productivity, strength, and sweetness, qualities that encapsulated her multifaceted role in Israel's history. Introduced in Judges 4, she is presented as a notable leader who defied traditional gender roles of her time. While the biblical narrative does not specify her lineage, it mentions that she was a prophetess and held court under the Palm of Deborah, where the Israelites came to her for judgment. This setting is significant; it highlights a public space where she exercised authority and earned respect from her peers. By doing so, Deborah became not only a judicial figure but also a source of spiritual guidance during a time when instability and fear loomed large.

To comprehend Deborah's leadership, one must examine the underlying societal attitudes towards women in ancient Israel. The patriarchal structure prevalent in their society often relegated women to the domestic sphere. Despite this, women like Deborah, Jael, and Hannah found ways to assert their influence and agency, often transcending societal norms. Deborah, in her capacity as a prophetess, bridged the domains of spiritual and military leadership. As a prophetess, she conveyed God's messages to her people, guiding them through their moral and spiritual dilemmas. This role positioned her as a spiritual intermediary, fulfilling a significant need for divine counsel in a time of crisis.

Deborah's role was not merely ceremonial; she actively participated in the military affairs of her country. She summoned Barak, a military commander, and compelled him to gather an army to confront the Canaanite oppression led by Sisera. This call to arms underscores her decisiveness and bravery. It is noteworthy that she did not hesitate to take bold action, revealing her unwillingness to accept the status quo if it meant allowing injustice to flourish. Her prophetic insight recognized not only the imminent threat posed by Sisera but also the need for collective action to reclaim their identity as God's chosen people.

Moreover, Deborah's leadership can be understood in the context of Israel's interpretation of divine authority. As someone who operated with divine endorsement, she symbolized hope and courage for the Israelites, instilling in them a sense of purpose. Her actions were rooted in faith, depicting a clear connection between spiritual leadership and engagement in the sociopolitical crises of the time. This dynamic reveals that women, although marginalized, held pivotal roles within the clan and community structures. They were integral to both the familial and spiritual realms, as well as international relations and warfare, even if their contributions were often obscured in historical accounts.

As observed through Deborah's story, the critical juncture at which she emerged illustrates that God's calling is not constrained by gender. The biblical narrative encourages believers to recognize the diverse ways women can operate within God's plans. God's selection of Deborah, a woman, to be a leader during a crucial time in history serves as a reminder that leadership qualities such as courage, discernment, and wisdom are not bound by societal norms or expectations.

This radical inclusivity emerges from the understanding that the biblical authors aimed to highlight the sovereignty of God in the establishment of leaders and judges. In a culture where authority and rule often resided primarily with men, God's choice of Deborah speaks to a progressive theology that transcends cultural norms. This understanding can foster a more inclusive view of leadership within both historical and contemporary faith contexts, urging communities to embrace leadership structures that honor divine gifts above human-made limitations.

Deborah's legacy can also be seen in the aftermath of her leadership during the battle against Sisera. In Judges 5, the Song of Deborah celebrates her military success and the pivotal role women played in Israel's history, showcasing that her influence extended beyond her immediate actions. The song's verses highlight the interconnectedness of individual and collective identity, resonating with themes of victory, empowerment, and divine intervention. It invites readers to reflect on how shared experiences can shape community narratives, encouraging women of faith today to find strength in communal and spiritual bonds.

By contextualizing Deborah's life and leadership, we can derive compelling lessons relevant to women in our modern society. Like Deborah, contemporary women face their unique challenges and societal pressures, yet they are called to find their voices and engage with their communities. Emulating Deborah's courage means advocating for justice, standing firm in faith, and leading with compassion amidst adversity.

Finally, understanding Deborah in context invites an exploration of the narratives surrounding her contemporaries, both male and female, within the biblical text. Comparatively, women like Hannah and Jael also navigated the patriarchal complexities of their time. Their stories, alongside Deborah's, collectively portray a tapestry of resilience, leadership, and divine purpose. Each narrative becomes a thread in a larger story of faith that urges readers to recognize and honor the diversity of God's calling upon women throughout history.

In conclusion, Deborah's story is rich with lessons that transcend time. By understanding her context, both socially and forward-thinking in faith, we can appreciate her role not just as a historical figure but as an archetype of leadership that continues to inspire. Her narrative encourages every woman, like Hannah, to embrace her voice, act with courage, and lead with conviction, knowing that her contributions are essential for fulfilling a divine purpose within her family and community. Thus, Deborah serves as more than just a historical character; she stands as a beacon of strength, illuminating pathways for future generations to walk in faith and purpose.

Courage in Leadership

Deborah's leadership in the Book of Judges stands out not just for the position she held but for the essence of her character, an embodiment of courage and wisdom. In a time when Israel was under oppression, Deborah rose as a prophetess and a judge, guiding her people with a blend of strength and insight. Her story is a testament to what it means to lead with courage, and it offers profound lessons for women today who are called to step into their authority, much like Hannah did in her role as a mother.

Courage, often defined as the mental or moral strength to venture, persevere, and withstand danger, fear, or difficulty, is a cornerstone of effective leadership. Deborah's actions exemplified this quality at every turn. She was not only willing to interpret God's message for the Israelites but also to take decisive action against their oppressors. Her confidence in God's command and her ability to guide Barak, the military leader, to assemble the troops reveal the depths of her conviction. Unlike many leaders who may falter in uncertainty, Deborah's unwavering faith instilled courage in those around her, ultimately leading them to victory.

Courage in leadership, however, is not limited to fearless action; it also encompasses the wisdom to understand when and how to act. Deborah's ability to listen to God and interpret His will showcases her spiritual insight, guiding her decisions in a manner that was not only strategic but deeply rooted in faith. When Barak hesitated to go to battle without her, it was Deborah's wisdom and strength of character that drove her to accompany him. Her presence on the battlefield was both a source of strength for Barak and a testament to her commitment to her people's cause. This demonstrated that true leadership does not shy away from challenges but embraces them with an authoritative presence that encourages others to follow.

In drawing parallels between Deborah and Hannah, we see how both women reflected the essence of courage in their respective circumstances. Hannah, though not a leader in the traditional political or military sense, exhibited her own unique strength in a societal role that demanded resilience and bravery. She faced deep personal challenges, battling the stigma of infertility and the emotional turmoil that accompanied it. It was her unwavering faith and fervent prayer that positioned her to not only seek a blessing for herself but also to take bold steps in dedicating her son Samuel to God's service. Hannah's act of surrender and faith echoes Deborah's own courage in trusting God's plan. Both women positioned themselves to be vessels for a greater purpose, leading by example in their unique contexts. Hannah's determination to pray for a child, despite her anguish, resembles Deborah's commitment to seek guidance from God for the nation of Israel. Their stories teach us that courage is not singularly manifested in overt actions but can also manifest in unwavering faith and quiet determination.

Deborah navigated a patriarchal society where women were typically relegated to the background, yet she stepped into her role as a leader without apology. Her story illustrates how leadership transcends gender norms and societal expectations. She demonstrated that women can possess authority and make significant impacts, paving the way for others to follow. In contrast, Hannah's strength lay in her role as a mother; she influenced Samuel, a future prophet and leader, through her fervent dedication and unwavering faith. While Deborah led from the frontlines, Hannah's leadership emerged from the intimate space of home, illustrating that courage can manifest in various forms.

The duality of Deborah's and Hannah's strength reveals a broader truth about women's leadership. Both women exemplified how courage requires vulnerability. Deborah, by taking risks in commanding an army, opened herself to potential failure and criticism. Hannah, too, showed her vulnerability in her prayers and in the quiet strength she wielded in raising Samuel. This vulnerability is not weakness; rather, it highlights an essential truth: courage often requires stepping beyond our comfort zones and embracing the unknown.

Moreover, both women's stories provoke contemplation on the nature of authority itself. Deborah's authority was recognized by her people; they sought her counsel and guidance, highlighting how effective leaders cultivate relationships built on respect and trust. In a similar vein, Hannah's authority over Samuel was rooted in the nurturing love and intentional upbringing she provided him, exemplifying how influence often stems from deep personal connections. Their stories compel women to embrace their unique forms of authority, whether in the workplace, community, or home.

Deborah's strategic courage can teach us valuable lessons about collaboration and building alliances. Her relationship with Barak exemplifies how leaders can empower others to rise to the occasion. Rather than seeking to dominate, Deborah worked alongside Barak, demonstrating that true leadership is not about exerting power but fostering teamwork. Hannah, too, played an important role in Samuel's life by actively engaging in his upbringing, ensuring he understood his divine purpose. Their legacies remind us that great leaders inspire and enable others to fulfill their potential.

Throughout history and even in present times, women in leadership positions often face scrutiny and are subject to higher expectations than their male counterparts. Deborah's story serves as an encouraging reminder that perseverance against societal challenges is possible. She became a beacon of hope during Israel's darkest periods, showing that women can lead with authority and integrity. Similarly, Hannah's story of perseverance in prayer and her eventual fulfillment serves as an implicit encouragement for women who feel their circumstances limit their potential. Both women are emblematic of the resilience, faith, and courage needed for meaningful leadership.

In a world where women continue to find their voices, the lessons drawn from Deborah and Hannah resonate deeply. Courage in leadership is not solely about being at the forefront of a movement; it is also about understanding our influence within smaller spheres and using that to sow seeds of change. Women are called to recognize their strengths, whether they be in the public eye or within the sacred walls of their homes.

As women continue to step into leadership roles, we must learn from the courage demonstrated by Deborah. Boldness empowered her to challenge societal norms, leading her people toward victory and setting a precedent for future generations of women. We must remember, too, that being a leader like Hannah doesn't mean stepping outside of home responsibilities but finding ways to influence and nurture future generations. The courage to lead, and to do so with wisdom, remains as relevant today as it was in Deborah's time. Women like her and Hannah illuminate a path forward, encouraging contemporary women to embrace their unique strengths, their rightful places of influence, and their deep reservoirs of courage.

As we honor their legacies, we lay groundwork for future generations of women leaders who will undoubtedly face their own challenges but can draw upon the rich examples of courage and strength established by those who came before them. In this contemporary story of leadership, let us remember that courage does not always look the same; it can be the shouting battle cry of Deborah or the quiet, determined prayers of Hannah. Both women exemplified the essence of what it means to lead and inspire others, teaching us that no matter the form, courage is rooted in unwavering faith, strength of character, and the willingness to embrace authority and influence for a greater purpose. Their stories call out to women everywhere, encouraging us to rise to our leadership potential, to influence those around us, and to step boldly into the calling that has been set before us.

Deborah as a Model for Modern Women

In the annals of biblical history, the figure of Deborah emerges as a beacon of leadership and strength, embodying qualities that modern women can draw inspiration from as they navigate their own paths in spheres of influence. As a prophetess, a warrior, and a judge, Deborah not only occupied a unique space among her contemporaries but also transcended her era, offering lessons that remain relevant today. Her story serves as both a guiding light and a challenge to women who aspire to lead, emphasizing the importance of embracing one's gifts while leading with courage and conviction.

Deborah lived during a time when Israel was under oppression, facing the formidable threat of Sisera, the commander of Jabin's army. Despite the shadow of despair that loomed over her people, Deborah emerged as a fearless leader. Her story begins in the Book of Judges, where we find her seated under the palm tree of Deborah, offering counsel and judgment to the people. This image is striking: a woman, both revered and respected, holding court in a male-dominated society. Through her actions, she demonstrates that true leadership transcends gender. It is based on one's ability to inspire, guide, and deliver justice.

For contemporary women, Deborah's story serves as a powerful reminder that leadership is not confined to specific roles or titles but is rooted in the ability to influence others positively. In today's world, women often find themselves balancing multiple roles, from professional responsibilities to familial obligations. Yet, like Deborah, they can harness their unique experiences and perspectives as assets in their leadership journey. By acknowledging their capacities and embracing the breadth of their potential, women can emerge as competent and confident leaders in various domains.

One of the most compelling aspects of Deborah's leadership is her decision to take action in a moment of crisis. When she summoned Barak, the military leader of Israel, and charged him with leading an army against Sisera, it was not merely a call to arms; it was an assertion of her authority and vision. Deborah understood the stakes. She recognized that the survival of her people depended on decisive action, and she did not hesitate to step forward. In a similar vein, modern women in leadership roles must be willing to assert themselves when faced with challenges, advocating for their beliefs and standing firm in their convictions, even when the odds seem insurmountable.

Moreover, Deborah's collaboration with Barak is a powerful illustration of the importance of teamwork in effective leadership. She encouraged him not just to lead but also to believe in his capacity to achieve victory. This dynamic partnership exemplifies how leaders can empower those around them. Deborah's belief in Barak's potential allowed him to rise to the occasion, illustrating that great leaders empower others to succeed. Thus, today's women in leadership must remember the value of collaboration, understanding that success is rarely a solo endeavor. By cultivating relationships based on trust and mutual respect, they can foster environments where all voices are heard and collective strengths are maximized.

Deborah's story also reveals the importance of faith in her leadership journey. She was guided by divine instruction and trusted in God's plan, even when faced with daunting challenges. Her faith was not passive; it was an active force that propelled her forward. In a world rife with uncertainty, the same principle holds true for modern women.

Drawing strength from their beliefs, whether spiritual or personal, can serve as a compass in navigating complex situations. Just as Deborah leaned into her faith to guide her actions, contemporary leaders can harness their core values and principles to remain grounded as they chart their course, especially during turbulent times.

Furthermore, Deborah exemplifies resilience, an essential trait for any effective leader. Despite the immense pressure and the potential for failure, she did not waver in her commitment. She understood that true leadership involves facing adversity head-on. This message resonates deeply with modern women who may encounter obstacles in their leadership journeys. Whether it's gender bias, societal expectations, or personal challenges, Deborah's unwavering spirit inspires women to persist. It invites them to view setbacks as opportunities for growth rather than insurmountable barriers.

In exploring Deborah's multifaceted nature, we see that she was not solely a warrior; she was also a nurturer and a source of wisdom. This balance is crucial for contemporary women leading in various settings. In a corporate environment, for example, the ability to be authoritative while also compassionate is invaluable. Deborah's ability to combine strength with empathy is a lesson for all leaders today. It challenges the stereotype that leaders must embody a singular trait or persona. Instead, it celebrates the complexity of leaders, affirming that one can be both strong and caring, decisive and relatable.

As we draw parallels between Deborah's story and the journeys of modern women, it is essential to acknowledge the barriers that still exist today. Women often encounter challenges in their quest for leadership positions, facing obstacles rooted in cultural expectations and systemic inequalities. However, inspired by Deborah, women can approach these barriers with courage and resolve. By asserting their value and seeking opportunities to lead, they can gradually reshape narratives around women in leadership. Deborah's defiance of societal norms offers a blueprint for doing just that; she reminds us that history can be rewritten through decisive action and unwavering faith.

The story of Deborah also invites reflection on the concept of legacy. As she led her people to victory, she secured her place in history as a revered figure. For modern women, the question arises: what kind of legacy do they wish to leave? Every decision and action contributes to this legacy. By leading authentically, grounded in their values, women can carve their paths while also paving the way for future generations.

In recent years, many contemporary women have taken inspiration from historical figures like Deborah. They have risen in various fields – politics, business, and advocacy – making their voices heard and their visions known. These women embody the leadership qualities that Deborah exemplified, embracing their gifts and breaking barriers. As more rise to positions of influence, they not only honor Deborah's legacy but expand it, adding depth and breadth to the narrative of women in leadership.

The work of modern women leaders also highlights the truth that leadership is an ongoing journey, one characterized by learning and growth. Deborah did not become a leader overnight; her role evolved as she responded to the needs of her people and embraced her destiny. For contemporary women, the journey entails developing skills, seeking mentorship, and remaining open to change. By cultivating a mindset of continuous growth, women can navigate their unique leadership paths with grace and confidence.

As we draw this exploration of Deborah as a model for contemporary women to a close, it is essential to recognize that every woman has the potential for leadership within her. Deborah's story serves as a clarion call, urging women to embrace their strengths and rise to the challenges before them. Whether in their families, communities, workplaces, or social spheres, women are called to lead with conviction, guided by faith, resilience, and a commitment to empowering others.

In essence, Deborah is not merely a character in a historical narrative; she is a timeless reminder of what it means to lead with strength, vision, and heart. Her life encourages modern women to seek out their own leadership opportunities, to collaborate and uplift those around them, and to remain steadfast in the face of adversity. As they navigate the complexities and joys of leadership, they can look to Deborah as a source of inspiration, empowered to write their own stories of strength and influence.

Deborah's legacy is a testament to the power of women leading with purpose. It is a legacy that resonates through time, inviting women everywhere to rise, lead, and inspire. Whether in small groups or on significant platforms, women can carry forth the mantle of leadership, guided by the principles and lessons embodied by Deborah, the ultimate warrior, prophetess, and advocate for justice. Let this call to action reverberate in the hearts of all women, encouraging them to embrace their gifts, trust their instincts, and step forward into their leadership roles, confident in the knowledge that they, like Deborah, can change the course of history.

MARY'S ACCEPTANCE: THE COURAGE OF A NEW BEGINNING

The Call of Mary

Mary's reaction to the angel's message is an extraordinary moment in the pages of the New Testament, encapsulating the essence of faith, courage, and acceptance. When the angel Gabriel appeared to her with a life-altering announcement, Mary was confronted with a call that would forever change her destiny and the course of history. She was merely a young woman, likely in her early teens, living in a small town called Nazareth. In that fleeting moment, her world spiraled into a whirlwind of uncertainty and awe. The angel's proclamation that she would conceive a child by the Holy Spirit immediately thrust her into a reality far beyond her comprehension, a reality pregnant with both promise and peril.

The courage Mary displayed in accepting this heavenly call deserves acknowledgment and reflection, especially in the context of other women in the Bible who faced their own daunting challenges. Mary's acceptance mirrors the journey of Hannah, whose narrative of fierce devotion and longing resonates deeply. Both women exemplified an admirable blend of faith and strength, navigated societal expectations, and ultimately embraced their unique roles in divine plans.

For Mary, the angel's greeting – "Greetings, favored one! The Lord is with you" – was both a blessing and a declaration of her role in the unfolding of God's promise. Yet it was Mary's internal struggle with the implications of such an announcement that reflects her humanity. "Confused and disturbed," she pondered what the angel could mean. This initiation into uncertainty exposes a universal theme: the tension between the extraordinary and the ordinary, between the fear of the unknown and the call to step forward in faith. Even the most faithful among us encounter confusion and fear when confronted with God's plans, underscoring the shared human experience of grappling with divine directives.

In contrast, Hannah's story presents another form of acceptance rooted in longing and perseverance. Like Mary, Hannah faced the stigma of barrenness, a source of deep anguish in her life as she longed for a child. Her heartfelt prayers, amplified by her sorrow, reached the heavens, culminating in a pivotal moment when she promised God that if He granted her a son, she would dedicate him to the Lord's service. Both women shared an extraordinary calling: Hannah's commitment to motherhood, even amidst her trials, and Mary's acceptance of the miraculous task of bringing the Savior into the world. Hannah's distress and desperation for a child resonate deeply with Mary's initial fears and doubts. Yet both women chose to surrender their fears and accept the paths set before them, trusting that they were not alone, no matter how daunting the journey became. Hannah's faith was wrought through tears, her acceptance forged in the fires of longing, while Mary's faith was punctuated by wonder and uncertainty, yet equally compelling. They both embraced the intricacies of their respective roles as mothers, displaying resilience that transcended the circumstances of their lives.

When Mary, armed with the weight of her revelation, spoke her remarkable words, "I am the Lord's servant," she embodied acceptance that resonates through the ages. This statement, simple yet profound, reflects a resolute commitment to God's will even when the implications were immense. This is a moment of courageous acceptance; it is as if Mary placed her trust in the divine plan, notwithstanding any social ramifications she might face as an unwed mother in her community. In this light, her response is a radical departure from societal expectations and norms, invoking a spirit of courage that resonates with Hannah's own battle against societal stigma tied to her barrenness.

It is essential to consider the context in which Mary lived. In a patriarchal society that placed immense value on women's roles as mothers and wives, her acceptance of this calling was laden with potential peril. She risked her reputation, her familial relationships, and perhaps her very life. Nevertheless, she articulated her consent with grace, demonstrating that true courage often entails stepping into the unknown with faith in God's promise of purpose. The very act of saying "yes" to such a profound calling mirrors Hannah's transformation from sorrow to empowerment as she dedicated her son Samuel, fulfilling her vow to God with tenacity and devotion.

The parallels between Mary and Hannah extend beyond their roles as mothers into the fabric of their faith journeys. Both women responded to God's calling amidst the crucible of challenge and societal pressures. Each of them symbolizes the struggle between personal desires and divine purposes. Mary's journey, like Hannah's, emphasizes the idea that acceptance can take many forms, and it is often suffused with both joy and pain. The acceptance of a new beginning, whether it is the romanticized moment of a miraculous pregnancy or the weary, prayerful pleas of a heart heavy with unfulfilled hopes, reveals the raw vulnerability and strength intrinsic to the experiences of women.

Acceptance, therefore, becomes a recurring theme as we weave through the stories of these two women. In their journeys, both Hannah and Mary faced cultural expectations and emotional turmoil while standing firm in their resolve to fulfill God's calling. Mary's readiness to embrace challenge, rooted in faith, reflects a conviction that God equips those He calls. With each prayer and each response, they laid the cornerstone of future generations who would inherit their legacies of faith and courage, thus transforming the narratives of divine calling into profound testimonies of hope.

Mary's acceptance was not a one-time declaration but a continual journey of courage. From her initial acceptance of the angel's message to the profound experiences of motherhood, she displayed ongoing faith that manifested through moments of clarity and joy as well as doubt and difficulty. The weight of being the mother of Jesus was not just a privilege; it was an immense responsibility that required her to remain steadfast amidst the multitude of challenges she would face. Pregnant before marriage, she would endure whispers and judgment within her community. Each of these challenges called for courage, a theme echoed in Hannah's own journey through the layers of societal expectation and personal anguish.

Hannah's acceptance of her calling brought forth not merely the joy of a child but also the promise of dedicating her son to a divine purpose. Her faith propelled her from the depths of despair into a renewed identity as a mother of a prophet. Similarly, Mary's acceptance ushered in the profound realization of her role as the Mother of God, a calling laden with divine significance and, at times, the weight of suffering. Both acceptance narratives encourage us to reflect on our responses to the calls we receive in our lives. Whether prompted by personal yearning or divine intervention, they beckon us toward acceptance that shapes not only our destinies but the legacies we leave behind.

As Mary embarked on her journey of motherhood, there was the necessity of resilience, a quality that infuses mothers throughout the ages with strength. The call of Mary was a summons to embrace motherhood not only as a physical act of giving birth but also as spiritual nurturing, guiding her child, Jesus, through a tumultuous world. In Hannah's narrative, each moment of her son Samuel's life was cradled in prayer, sacrifice, and intent, further amplifying the significance of nurturing one's calling with faith and devotion.

Mary's acceptance imparted courage to a generation of believers. Her Magnificat reverberates as a spirit of praise, a powerful declaration that embodies the essence of accepting the divine in the midst of hardship. "My soul magnifies the Lord, and my spirit rejoices in God my Savior," she proclaimed, illustrating the transcendent nature of faith, hope, and courage. Similarly, Hannah's prayer of thanksgiving upon Samuel's birth resonates through generations, reverberating the theme of redemption through faith. Both women not only exemplified formidable courage but also served as vessels of faith that would influence countless lives.

Reflecting on the lessons gleaned from both Mary and Hannah, we recognize the profound nature of courage inherent in acceptance. It challenges us to reevaluate how we respond to our calls, those gentle nudges that beckon us toward courage and commitment, whether they are intertwined with motherhood, vocation, or acts of service. The essence of their stories inspires us to confront our fears, relinquish our doubts, and move forward into the unknown with faith-equipped hearts. The challenge of accepting one's calling, whether as mother, leader, or servant, is universal. As women, we carry the legacies of those who walked similar paths before us, women of immense faith who spoke courage into the heart of their circumstances. Hannah and Mary continue to invite us into the exploration of what it means to embrace our unique calls amid uncertainty, lending strength to our own journeys through the threads of shared experiences.

In the tapestry of womanhood, there lies an intrinsic courage that unites us in the pursuit of our calls, whether they be ordinary or divine. Hannah and Mary emanate a bravery that is beyond themselves; it is a legacy of unwavering faith and acceptance that stretches across history, ultimately inviting generations to ponder their own unique callings with courage and hope. Each woman is a testament to the power of saying "yes" to possibilities beyond comprehension, charting paths for others to walk in faith and acceptance of their own unique destinies. As we reflect on the courageous acceptance of Mary and Hannah, we are reminded that the journey may not always be easy, but with faith, hope, and a resolute heart, we can embrace the new beginnings that stretch before us.

Stepping into the Unknown

In the story of Mary, we encounter a young woman faced with an unimaginable reality. The angel Gabriel's announcement reverberates through her life like a thunderclap, shaking the very foundations of her existence and propelling her into a future cloaked in uncertainty. From this moment, Mary must embrace the daunting prospect of stepping into the unknown, a theme that resonates deeply with Hannah's own experiences, as both women are called to navigate the complexities of their faith and the divine plans laid out before them.

Mary's predicament is extraordinary, yet her response is profoundly human. The weight of the angel's message that she will conceive the Son of God brings forth a whirlwind of emotions: joy, fear, confusion, and an overwhelming sense of responsibility. In the face of her societal context, a young unmarried woman pregnant by the Holy Spirit could expect ostracization at best, and worse, stoning for what would be perceived as an act of immorality. Yet it is precisely this scenario that demands her courage. Like Hannah, who faced the stigma of barrenness and the ridicule of Peninnah, Mary too stands at the forefront of public scrutiny, her faith required to shield her from the doubts that threaten to envelop her.

Both women embody the courageous spirit of acceptance in the face of overwhelming odds, but their journeys illuminate distinct paths toward stewardship. Hannah, in her desperation, fervently prays for a child, promising to dedicate him to the Lord. Her tears and pleas signal her unwavering commitment and trust in God's timing. Meanwhile, Mary's leap of faith springs from an acknowledgment of her own limitations, as she submits her will to that of the divine. "I am the Lord's servant," she proclaims, illustrating her willingness to accept a path that is not only fraught with difficulty but infused with sanctity. This attitude inspires us to confront the uncertainties in our own lives with faith, understanding that divine plans often come wrapped in challenges.

Stepping into the unknown requires an unwavering trust in God's character and His promises. Mary's acceptance is not merely an affirmation of her role in a grand narrative; it is an act of radical faith that resonates through time. Her declaration serves as a beacon for all who struggle with the unpredictable nature of life. Like Hannah, who journeyed through seasons of heartache and yearning, Mary invites us to consider what it means to walk with God when the road ahead appears obscure.

Both Mary and Hannah exhibit a remarkable openness to God's leading. Hannah's dedication of her son, Samuel, to the temple life reflects a desire for her child's purpose to be greater than her own dreams for motherhood. In this, she allows God to guide the trajectory of Samuel's future, embodying a willingness to surrender control. Mary echoes this surrender, embracing her role in a divine story that transcends even the constraints of her understanding. Their shared humility underscores a profound truth: stepping into the unknown often requires relinquishing certain comforts and embracing divine intentions beyond our immediate perceptions.

As we delve deeper into Mary's story, we must consider the nature of faith itself within the realm of uncertainty. Faith, unlike certainty, demands action without a guarantee of outcome. Hannah's faith was displayed through her persistent prayers and vows, her emotional transparency to God serving as a testament to her trust. She desired a son but had to release that desire into God's hands. Mary, too, showcases the essence of faith as she accepts a task that could bring about significant hardship. This sense of trust, an essential ingredient in stepping into the unknown, prompted Hannah to continue praying and waiting, and it emboldened Mary to step forward into a role that could change the course of history.

The two women also faced the burdens of societal judgment, each enduring their own form of ostracism. Hannah endured the taunts of her rival, Peninnah, who mocked her inability to conceive, while Mary confronted the stigma of unwed motherhood. Their parallel experiences reveal a deeper truth that stepping into the unknown often invites criticism and misunderstanding. Each woman, however, found strength in their unwavering commitment to God's purpose, providing an inspirational model for those of us navigating our own paths.

Hannah teaches us that while the unknown may appear daunting, there is transformative power in sincere prayer and desperation. Her willingness to voice her pain before God draws parallels to Mary's quiet, steadfast acceptance. Both women become vessels of something far greater than themselves, a truth that inspires us to contemplate the significance of our own journeys into the uncertainties of life. Moreover, stepping into the unknown challenges us to look beyond our immediate fears and desires. Mary's acceptance was not devoid of questions; she too wondered how such a miraculous event could happen. "How will this be?" she asks the angel when confronted with her unexpected reality. Even in her questioning, there is an undercurrent of belief; it is the interplay of doubt and faith that adds depth to her story. Similarly, Hannah's anguished pleas signify a yearning for clarity and assurance in a turbulent sea of heartache. Their journeys remind us that questioning is not antithetical to faith but often a crucial step toward a deeper understanding of God's plans.

As we reflect upon the narratives of these two women, we encounter an invitation to confront the uncertainties in our own lives, those moments when the way forward is unclear and the future feels daunting. Hannah and Mary exemplify the belief that each step into the unknown holds the potential for profound blessings, urging us to trust the divine guidance that accompanies our journeys. Their narratives become a powerful testament to the importance of maintaining faith when circumstances feel insurmountable.

In the crucible of uncertainty, both women experienced a transformation, aligning their lives with God's purpose. Hannah ultimately finds joy and fulfillment in Samuel's birth, but her journey does not end there; she joyfully dedicates him to God, marking a pivotal moment of surrender. Likewise, Mary gives birth to Jesus, embodying the divine promise of redemption and grace for all humanity. Their stories compel us to consider the significance of surrendering our own aspirations, allowing God to weave our lives into a bigger tapestry of purpose.

Stepping into the unknown challenges us to examine the way we respond to unforeseen circumstances. Fear and doubt can overshadow our path, but faith empowers us to move forward with courage. Hannah's fervent prayers provide an example of resilience, while Mary's acceptance serves as a model of trust, both pivotal components for anyone facing trials. Each woman's story stands as a testament to the truth that although the unknown can be frightening, divine purpose is often found within the challenges we face.

As we step into the unknown realms of our lives, we are reassured that we do not walk alone. Through Hannah's pleas for a child and Mary's acceptance of motherhood, we find echoes of our own struggles, dreams, and fears. They become allies in our journeys, reminding us that even when faced with uncertainty, there is an opportunity for growth and a deeper relationship with the divine. Their narratives encourage us to confront our unknowns with a spirit of courage, faith, and trust, both in ourselves and in the divine plan at work.

In acknowledging the profound uncertainty that often defines our paths, we glean valuable lessons from the stories of Hannah and Mary. As we seek to understand God's purpose for our lives, we are reminded of the importance of faith in the midst of confusion. Both women exemplify the beauty of stepping into the unknown, showing us that surrender, courage, and an open heart can lead to extraordinary blessings beyond our comprehension.

Let us, like Hannah and Mary, respond to the whispers of our callings with grace and courage. May we embrace the unknown, trusting that our steps, illuminated by faith and guided by purpose, will lead us to transformative experiences that reshape not only our lives but the lives of those around us. The legacy of these women becomes our own as we navigate the complexities of our journeys, igniting a deeper commitment to our faith and a willingness to step boldly into whatever lies ahead.

The Legacy of Acceptance

In the tapestry of biblical narratives, few stories shine as brightly as that of Mary, the humble young woman chosen for an extraordinary purpose. Her acceptance of an angelic message forever altered the course of history. This subchapter delves deep into "The Legacy of Acceptance," exploring the enduring impact of Mary's courageous decision and how it reverberates through the centuries, encouraging each of us to embrace our own journeys with acceptance and grace.

To fully appreciate the significance of Mary's acceptance, we must first understand the context of her life. Living in a society bound by strict cultural norms, her situation was a perilous one. A young woman, betrothed and yet an unexpected announcement looming over her, a child conceived by the Holy Spirit. Her world was turned upside down, with her future hanging in the balance. Yet, amidst uncertainty and potential isolation, Mary did not falter. Instead, she responded with a simple yet profound declaration: "I am the Lord's servant. May your word to me be fulfilled" (Luke 1:38, NIV). This acceptance was more than mere acknowledgment; it was an act of tremendous faith and courage.

Mary's acceptance serves as a cornerstone of her legacy, one that transcends her immediate circumstance. The ripple effect of her decision can be traced through generations, inspiring countless individuals to embrace their own unique paths. For those who follow in her footsteps, Mary's story is emblematic of the profound impact that acceptance can have, not only on our lives but on the lives of others as well.

Acceptance, as modeled by Mary, is not just about passivity; it is an active engagement with God's will. When Mary accepted the angel's message, she took on the incredible responsibility of nurturing and raising the Son of God. This was no small task, and her legacy lies not only in the birth of Jesus but in her unwavering faith throughout His life. From the moment she said "yes," she became a pivotal figure in a larger story, one that would influence the course of humanity.

The influence of Mary's acceptance is evident in the lives of women throughout the Bible. Take Hannah, whose story we have examined. Hannah's journey was marked by deep anguish and a desperate plea for children. When she finally accepted her role and vowed to dedicate her son Samuel to the Lord, she did so with grace. Hannah's acceptance of her journey – filled with pain, heartache, and eventual joy – demonstrated that surrender and courage coexist beautifully in the journey of life. Both Hannah and Mary exemplified how both pain and joy can lead to something greater than oneself. They became vessels through which God's narrative unfolded, and their legacies reflect the power of acceptance.

As we traverse through generations, we see the effects of acceptance illustrated profoundly by women like Esther. Faced with the daunting prospect of risking her life to save her people, Esther, too, embraced her calling with courage. Her acceptance came at a tremendous personal cost, yet it resulted in her being an instrument of deliverance for the Israelites. The echo of her bravery and acceptance can be felt even today, as it has empowered women to speak out and stand firm in the face of adversity. Esther's and Mary's stories remind us that acceptance can be an act of profound courage and can lead to transformative change for many.

The legacy of acceptance further extends into the New Testament, in the lives of women who surrounded Jesus during His earthly ministry. The woman at the well, for instance, is a poignant illustration of acceptance and transformation. When Jesus conversed with her, acknowledging her woundedness and dignity, He invited her to embrace a new identity, one rooted in truth and acceptance of God's love. Her acceptance of this new identity became a legacy of evangelism as she boldly shared her experience, leading many in her town to believe in Jesus. Such stories affirm that acceptance can liberate and empower, allowing individuals to redefine their self-worth and purpose.

We must acknowledge, too, that Mary's journey of acceptance was not without its challenges. The stigma surrounding her pregnancy, the doubts of those around her, and the pain of watching her son face unspeakable suffering were burdens that weighed heavily on her. Yet, through it all, Mary's steadfast acceptance became a source of strength, showcasing the extraordinary power of resilience. Her ability to trust in God's plan, despite the uncertainties, is a lesson for each of us. It reinforces that acceptance is not devoid of difficulty but a choice to trust and move forward in faith.

Throughout history, many women have drawn strength from Mary's example. Scriptural narratives often highlight the courage women display in the face of societal norms, inspiring generations to embrace their roles as catalysts for change. The legacy of acceptance is encapsulated in the countless stories of women who have faced their fears and embraced their challenges, driven by a desire to fulfill their God-given purpose. From the women in the early church to contemporary figures in faith communities, the call to accept one's circumstances and trust in God reverberates through time.

Moreover, the legacy of acceptance has implications not just for individuals but for communities and societies. When we accept ourselves and others with grace, we create an atmosphere of love and support. Mary's acceptance of her difficult path laid the groundwork for inclusivity, teaching us that acceptance fosters understanding. Just as Mary embraced her role and nurtured the Messiah, we too are called to cultivate a spirit of acceptance in our families, churches, and communities. By modeling Mary's behavior, we can inspire those around us to seek healing, love, and understanding.

In today's fast-paced world, the concept of acceptance may seem challenging. Societal pressures, expectations, and judgments can cloud our ability to accept not only ourselves but also the paths laid out for us by God. Yet, reflecting on Mary's story provides a clarion call to rise above these challenges. Her courage to accept her role as the mother of Jesus illuminates the transformative power of saying "yes" to God's calling. The legacy of acceptance is not meant to remain an abstract lesson; it beckons us to live it out in our daily interactions and relationships.

As we contemplate the essence of acceptance, it is essential to recognize that it often requires vulnerability. Just as Mary opened herself up to the uncertainties that lay ahead, we too are called to be vulnerable and trust in God's purpose for our lives. This vulnerability can forge deeper connections and foster a more dynamic faith community. Mary's acceptance illuminated the importance of communal relationships; her visit to Elizabeth encapsulated the beauty of shared journeys, friendship, and mutual encouragement. Her acceptance fostered bonds among women, reminding us of our collective role in nurturing one another's faith journeys.

Consider how acceptance can pave the way for reconciliation and healing. In a world plagued by division and strife, Mary's legacy invites us to embrace love and acceptance over judgment and separation. When we encounter individuals whose experiences differ vastly from our own, it is essential to approach these relationships with an open heart, just as Mary approached her divine calling. Her example encourages a radical acceptance of differences, giving us the courage to unite under a common purpose, sharing the love of Christ with a hurting world.

The powerful implications of Mary's acceptance extend beyond mere familial ties. They reach into the broader narrative of faith, encouraging us to embrace the unexpected twists of our own stories. Each of us is on a unique journey, filled with moments of uncertainty and challenges. In embracing acceptance, we open the door to growth and transformation. When we lean into God's promises, allowing His will to unfold, we navigate life's intricate pathways with a newfound sense of purpose and direction.

At its core, the legacy of acceptance calls each of us to surrender our desires, fears, and preconceptions to God. As we reflect upon Mary's journey, we recognize that acceptance is not a one-time event, but an ongoing process of faith. The challenges we face often require repeated commitments to accept God's plans, similar to how Mary continually chose to trust in God throughout the trials of her life. With each act of acceptance, we lay the foundation for a legacy that benefits not only ourselves but also those we encounter along the way.

Mary's acceptance transformed her life, but it also left an indelible mark on the hearts of generations. As we embrace our own call to accept, we join her legacy, stepping out into the world with a courage rooted in faith. We are reminded that our acceptance can serve as a beacon of hope, encouraging others to find their own strength in surrender.

In conclusion, the legacy of acceptance emerges as a powerful theme woven throughout the biblical narrative. Mary's courageous acceptance transformed her life and the lives of countless others. Her story encourages readers to seek their own path of acceptance with courage, trusting in God's greater plan. The lessons of Mary's acceptance resonate through time, inviting each of us to engage actively with our circumstances while demonstrating love and grace to those around us. As we cultivate a spirit of acceptance in our lives, we pave the way for healing, growth, and ultimately, a legacy that reflects the heart of God. The challenge lies before us: to embrace acceptance, trusting that our "yes" can transform not only our lives but the lives of generations to come.

ESTHER'S DARING: COURAGE IN CRISIS

Esther's Challenge

Esther's Challenge unfolds within the rich tapestry of her narrative, a saga woven with threads of bravery, faith, and the weight of destiny. In the heart of this story is the young woman who would rise as a queen, facing an incalculable crisis that not only threatened her own life but the future of her people. The book of Esther paints a picture of a grand palace, opulence, and privilege, but under the shimmering veneer lies a reality pregnant with danger and deception. It is within this crucible of crisis that Esther's true character emerges, inviting us to uncover the layers of her challenge.

At the cusp of her journey, Esther finds herself in the Persian palace, having been crowned queen. This moment, however, is far from the conclusion of her personal story; it is a juncture that sets her on a path fraught with peril. The edict of King Ahasuerus, fueled by the vengeful ambitions of Haman, threatens the annihilation of her people, the Jews. As a Jewish woman wed to a powerful Gentile king, Esther stands on the precipice of a deep chasm, the chasm between her safety as a queen and her loyalty to her kindred. The decision she faces transcends personal safety; it is a matter of survival for her entire community.

Esther's circumstances evoke parallels with Hannah's experience. Both women grapple with existential challenges that pull them between their desires and their roles within the framework of their lives. Hannah, in her barrenness, sought divine intervention and cried out for a son, vowing to dedicate him back to God. In her narrative, we witness her vulnerability, wrestling with grief and hope intertwined. Similarly, Esther's hope flickers amid the shadows of doubt as she contemplates the risks associated with approaching the king unbidden, a move that could very well lead to her death.

Esther's fear is palpable. She hesitates to reveal her identity as a Jew, knowing that the revelation could have dire consequences not only for her but for every person linked to her. Mordecai's words echo in her mind, solidified as both a challenge and a call to arms: "Who knows but that you have come to royal position for such a time as this?" It is this pivotal statement that shatters her paralysis, compelling her to confront the crisis head-on. The challenge before her is not merely a test of courage but a defining moment of purpose and identity.

Meanwhile, the court of Ahasuerus is a labyrinthine environment where intrigue and danger lurk around every corner. Position and power create alliances, but they also breed jealousy and treachery. Esther, although initially an outsider, must learn to navigate this delicate landscape. Her beauty and grace enhance her status as queen, yet they are inadequate defenses against the machinations of Haman. As she contemplates her identity, she must ask herself: Is she merely a queen, beset by luxury and leisure, or does her role ignite a deeper calling to advocate for her people?

The biblical narrative captures her evolution as she prepares for her fateful decision. There is a mounting tension as she requests her royal husband to host a banquet, a setting where she plans to divulge her identity and the impending doom facing her people. Esther must summon not only her courage but also her wisdom and empathy. The banquet, a seemingly innocuous gathering, becomes a microcosm of the larger battle for survival. In her willingness to speak up, Esther proves that her voice is a powerful instrument against tyranny.

Her challenge doesn't dissipate in that royal hall; rather, it burgeons. Esther's resolve is decisive yet delicate, a blend of strength and vulnerability. She steps into the limelight at the risk of her own life, knowing well that the king's favor can turn like the wind. She must carefully choose her words, balancing the weight of her revelation with the necessity of persuasion. This moment can be viewed as a threshold, one foot in the world of privilege, the other straddling the far riskier realm of her heritage. Behind Esther's composure lies the essence of her womanhood, a fierce love for her people paired with the quiet agony of uncertainty.

Her relationship with Mordecai enhances this complexity; the bond reminds us that the journey against adversity is seldom a solitary endeavor. It underscores the importance of community, a reflection of Hannah's own experience where she weaves her plea with faith, invoking divine support. Just as God answered Hannah, Esther too finds that divine orchestration plays a role in her extraordinary challenge.

Mordecai's encouragement becomes a cornerstone of Esther's strength. He serves as a reminder of the responsibility that comes with her position, asking her to consider her role in a fuller capacity. She is not just a queen draped in silk and gold; she is God's instrument, positioned at a critical juncture in history. This perspective reshapes her understanding of courage. It is not merely the absence of fear but the presence of purpose.

As we reflect on Esther's challenge, we recognize that the stakes are intensely personal yet profoundly communal. The peril of genocide hangs over her people as a cloud of doom, while her heart aches at the thought of losing her family, her friends, her identity. This duality speaks to the universal truth of women's experiences throughout time. In moments of adversity, women often find the weight of the world rests on their shoulders, just as it did for Hannah, who vowed that if her prayers were answered, her son would serve God all his life. Esther contemplates the very survival of her nation, echoing Hannah's desperate desire for lineage and legacy.

As the climax draws near, Esther fully embodies the transformation from vulnerability to empowerment. She finally has her moment, a reconciling of her dual identity as both a queen and a Jewess. This integral realization fuels her courage, and she boldly addresses the king, revealing her Jewish heritage and the plot against her people. The ensuing confrontation with Haman encapsulates the gravity of her decision; Esther's bravery catalyzes a profound shift, weakening the perpetrator of evil and weaving a narrative of divine justice.

In the aftermath of her courageous stand, the story takes a transformative turn. Haman's sinister plans unravel, leading to justice for the Jewish people. As a result, we are reminded that voicing one's truth can alter the course of history. Esther's journey is an inspiring testimony to the incredible impact one person can have in moments of greatest peril.

Furthermore, the celebration of her triumph invites reflection on how courage can manifest in diverse ways, ranging from whispering a prayer in agony to speaking boldly in a king's court. The narrative of Esther, like that of Hannah, invites us to find our own voice, urging us to acknowledge both our fears and our faith. Ultimately, it illuminates the connection between personal sacrifice and communal destiny, a poignant reminder of our interdependence as women navigating an often turbulent world.

Esther's challenge encapsulates the essence of courage in crisis, leaving us with a blueprint for facing our own trials. As we weave together her story with Hannah's, we uncover common threads of resilience, faith, and tenacity. Both women serve as beacons of hope, guiding us to confront our fears and realize that even amidst the darkest moments, we possess the potential to change the course of our own stories and those of others around us.

In this light, Esther's signature of bravery becomes a guiding inspiration, teaching us that profound courage does not arise from the absence of fear but from the willingness to act despite it. As we delve deeper into the narratives of women in the Bible, we are equipped not only with lessons from the past but with an understanding that their challenges transcend time, imparting wisdom that continually shapes our identities today.

The essence of their stories rests in the quiet yet powerful moments of challenge. They remind us that we, too, can carve a path of change through the storms we face. In a world that often dismisses women's voices, Esther's story, together with that of Hannah, stands as an enduring call to courage, urging us to rise amid uncertainty and to recognize our worth, influence, and capacity for impact. As we embrace our individual stories, we honor their legacies and commit to carrying their lessons into our own lives, reminding ourselves that we, like Esther, are here "for such a time as this."

The Importance of Strategic Thinking

Esther's bravery in confronting the king to save her people is a remarkable story of courage, but it is equally a tale of strategic thinking. The Book of Esther presents the actions of a woman who did not act on impulse or emotion alone; she exercised wisdom, foresight, and a keen awareness of her surroundings. This careful approach highlights the intrinsic link between courage and strategy, a theme that resonates through the lives of women of faith, including Hannah.

Hannah's story, a poignant account of a woman plagued by grief and longing, showcases a different kind of courage. Her journey through despair toward faith is marked by strategic choices as much as Esther's royal court maneuverings. Each woman faced unique challenges, yet both demonstrated the importance of strategic thinking in their respective battles. While Esther navigated political intrigue and personal risk, Hannah navigated her own spiritual and emotional turmoil, each employing foresight to bring about monumental change.

Esther's situation unfolded against the backdrop of a lavish Persian court, where appearances, alliances, and power dynamics dictated survival. She knew that her beauty alone could not sustain her; she needed a well-thought-out plan. When her cousin Mordecai presented her with the information that her people faced annihilation, Esther didn't rush into action. Instead, she took stock of her position as queen, recognizing both her privilege and the peril that came with it. She understood the weight of approaching the king without an invitation, a potentially fatal misstep. It was not merely her royal status that empowered her but also her ability to strategize her approach.

Esther called for a fast, gathering support from her people. She understood the power of unity and the importance of seeking divine guidance. In doing so, she equipped herself spiritually and emotionally, using foresight to bolster her resolve. Her fasting was not just an act of mourning but a calculated means to prepare her heart and mind for the imminent challenge. It demonstrated her understanding of the unseen forces at play, not just the human actors in the court but the underlying spiritual battle for her people's very existence.

Just as Esther prepared herself, Hannah's story reflects another form of strategic thinking. When faced with the taunts and provocations of Peninnah, she did not retaliate in anger. Rather, Hannah chose the path of prayer and supplication. Her deep anguish led her to the temple, where she poured out her heart to God, making a vow that if He granted her a son, she would dedicate him to the Lord's service. Hannah's strategic thinking lay in her understanding of her circumstances and her decision to align her desires with divine will.

When linked together, the stories of Hannah and Esther reveal that courage requires more than just a bold heart; it requires wisdom. This link takes on a deeper significance when we consider the outcomes of their strategies. Esther's bold request to the king unfolded in stages, with her initial banquets serving to build rapport and create a favorable environment for her eventual plea. She knew that great outcomes often require great patience, a quality both women exemplified.

Hannah, too, practiced patience. The years of silence, the cycle of shame, and the deep yearning for a child reached a transformative peak when she turned her grief into faith. Her vow became a strategic declaration of intent, understanding that a promise to God was both a commitment and a source of strength. When Eli, the priest, misunderstood her fervent prayers as drunkenness, Hannah patiently clarified her intentions, highlighting her understanding that communication is crucial not only in prayer but in the outcomes we seek.

The contrast between the potential consequences of rash decisions versus those made with foresight is stark in both narratives. Had Esther rushed to speak to the king without careful consideration of the right moment or the right words, she could have jeopardized not only her life but also the lives of her entire people. Her eventual articulation of the truth, delivered at the right time and with grace, transformed her from a passive bystander into an active agent of change. Her strategic thinking and measured approach did not dismantle her courage; it enhanced it.

Similarly, Hannah's careful navigation of her trials did not lessen her anguish; it gave her a framework within which to process her pain and articulate her needs. Her strategic approach was one of humility and seeking, demonstrating that true courage is often found in vulnerability. By focusing on what she could control, her own responses and her commitments, Hannah exemplified a deeply rooted wisdom that aligned her actions with God's purpose for her life.

Connecting the threads of these two narratives allows us to see the broader implications of strategic thinking in a spiritual context. Both women found themselves in circumstances beyond their control. They were thrust into roles where the stakes were incredibly high. Yet, where one might falter in fear, both Hannah and Esther turned their circumstances into opportunities for faith-driven action, leveraging their intelligence and emotional acuity to navigate through crises.

Esther's tactical choices reveal an understanding of human nature, particularly the insecurities of power. Knowing King Ahasuerus' personality, she employed a series of subtle yet bold moves, including strategically timed banquets. Such planning showcases her foresight; instead of bombarding the king with demands, she chose to engage him in an environment of warmth and celebration, ultimately leading him toward a moment when he would be more amenable to her request. In this way, she understood that courage without strategy could lead to folly, that the heart of her bravery was learning to think ahead, even amidst imminent danger.

Hannah, likewise, operated with an acute understanding of both the personal and divine. Her prayer was not one of mere desperation but a meticulous surrender, merging her needs with a proclamation of faith. Each plea was a calculated step toward reconciliation with God's greater plans. She recognized that God could be trusted with the very essence of her being, her maternal hopes, and that commitment transformed her prayers into a testimony of faithfulness.

The intersection of these stories positions strategic thinking as a groundbreaking principle for any follower of faith. For modern women wrestling with their own challenges, the wisdom gleaned from Esther and Hannah is powerful. It asserts that courage is not merely a one-time leap into unknown waters but a continual engagement in thoughtful preparation and prayerful intent. To face a crisis, whether personal or communal, is to recognize that foresight and an understanding of the already established narrative significantly influence the outcomes we seek.

The impact of their strategic choices ripples beyond their own lives. Esther's actions saved a nation; she altered the course of history through her reasoned yet courageous stands. The festival of Purim continues to honor her legacy, a testament to the power of one woman's strategic heart aligned with divine purpose. Hannah's legacy, too, does not end with her story; her son, Samuel, became a pivotal figure in Israel's history, leading the people with wisdom and prophetic insight.

As living testimonies of courage coupled with foresight, the lives of Esther and Hannah provide a framework for our own efforts in navigating the challenges and crises we face. Just as Esther took time to prepare herself and her environment before making her plea, we, too, must consider the power of our actions in faith. Our intentions should meld with well-thought-out responses to ensure that our courage does not manifest as reckless abandon but as inspired action born from wisdom.

Furthermore, the importance of strategic thinking transcends gender, reminding all of us, men and women alike, of our need to navigate life's complexities with discernment. In our relationships, in our workplaces, in our communities, and indeed, in our spiritual lives, may we cultivate a mindset that anticipates the needs of the moment and seeks wisdom in every decision.

By observing the deliberate steps taken by both Esther and Hannah throughout their experiences, we gain insights into the gift of time and preparation. They teach us that while courage propels us forward, it is our ability to think strategically that prepares the way. In the face of daunting circumstances, learning to pause, pray, and plan may prove to be the most significant acts of bravery we can offer.

In effect, strategic thinking is about connecting the dots in our stories, recognizing patterns, and choosing paths that align with our values. Just as Esther and Hannah did not merely react to their situations but engaged them with intention, we too can create spaces for divine intervention by first engaging our minds and hearts with focused foresight.

In conclusion, the importance of strategic thinking in the acts of courage cannot be overstated. Both Esther's royal ascent and Hannah's devotion illustrate that courage is often not just a matter of the heart but a melding of heart, mind, and spirit. Each woman illustrates that true bravery involves understanding the complexities of one's circumstances and responding with thoughtful, calculated action. The interplay of faith and strategy enriches the narratives of both women, offering critical lessons as we navigate our own eras of trial, adversity, and opportunity. Thus, may we glean inspiration from their stories, empowering ourselves to redefine what it means to be both courageous and wise in the face of life's challenges.

Communal Empowerment

Esther's story is not only one of individual bravery but also one that illuminates the power of community in times of crisis. In the heart of the tale, we find a young Jewish woman who, through her courage and strategic thinking, transformed the fate of her people. This subchapter will delve into the concept of communal empowerment and how Esther's choices resonate beyond her personal journey, reaching into the lives of her fellow Jews. The courage she displayed acts as a beacon, guiding individuals to reflect on their roles within their own communities, especially when faced with adversity.

When we consider the dire situation of the Jewish people in Persia, it becomes clear that Esther's bravery was amplified by the strength of those around her. Her ascent to the role of queen was not solely a personal triumph; it was a pivotal moment that set the stage for collective action. Esther demonstrated that individual strength, when supported by community solidarity, can yield transformative outcomes. The chorus of voices that rose up around her, Mordecai's unwavering support, and the fasting and prayers of the Jewish people provided a backdrop against which her courage was painted. In this narrative, we find a template for understanding how communal empowerment can galvanize individuals to rise in the face of crises.

Esther did not act in isolation. Her courage was rooted in the collective fear and desperation of her community, which faced the imminent threat of extermination. When Mordecai approached her with the weight of their impending doom, he reminded her that her royal position could serve a greater purpose. "For if you remain silent at this time, relief and deliverance for the Jews will arise from another place, but you and your father's family will perish" (Esther 4:14). It was a powerful reminder that her actions or inactions would reverberate throughout her community. The message was clear: Esther's individual choices had the potential to uplift or devastate an entire people.

In the face of this crisis, Esther chose not to retreat into the safety of her royal comforts. Instead, she embraced her identity as a Jew and recognized the responsibility that came with her position. This realization did not simply spring from her strength but was also deeply intertwined with the solidarity of her people. Esther's upcoming confrontation with King Ahasuerus was not just a solitary act of bravery; it was the culmination of collective efforts, prayer, and resolve. The Jewish community fasted and prayed for three days, demonstrating their support and their shared investment in the outcome. United in their hope and despair, they embodied the strength that comes when individuals commit to a common cause.

As we reflect on the significance of communal empowerment in Esther's context, it becomes essential to draw parallels to our own lives. In times of crisis, we must ask ourselves, who stands with us? How do we come together to support one another? The modern world often encourages us to act as isolated individuals, celebrating feats of personal achievement. However, Esther's story calls us to remember the vital role of community, the way it can amplify our voices and bolster our actions. Courage is a multi-faceted gem, and while it may be polished by individual acts, its true brilliance shines brightest when it is illuminated by the collective light of a community. Each person's bravery contributes to a shared tapestry of strength, where each thread, woven together, forms a larger narrative of resilience. Esther's decision to reveal her Jewish identity was steeped not just in her resolve but also in the prayers and hopes of countless others who stood with her. Readers are invited to consider this powerful intersection of individual and communal bravery in their own journeys.

When we gather for a singular purpose, we create an environment where collective courage flourishes. The festival of Purim, which emerged from this very narrative, serves as a celebration of this communal interdependence. It honors not only Esther's bravery but also the collective strength of the Jewish people who came together in a time of crisis. This annual celebration reinforces the importance of remembering our shared history and the struggles that shaped our identities. The remembrance acts as a reminder that we are stronger together, and actively participating in a community empowers us to confront challenges with renewed vigor.

Communal empowerment is not just about physical support; it encompasses emotional, spiritual, and psychological dimensions as well. In Esther's time, the cry for help was met with a powerful response, where shared grief transformed into a collective resolve. This synergy is crucial today, where isolation can be a byproduct of modern living. Esther's journey illustrates the necessity of leaning into community. In doing so, we open ourselves to the possibility of shared healing and mutual strength. As we navigate our own crises, whether personal, familial, or societal, we must not forget the power of collective action. Esther's story encourages us to connect with our communities, to foster relationships that deepen our commitments to one another. When faced with seemingly insurmountable odds, who will rally around us? How do we inspire those who may feel powerless? Strength lies not solely in the individual but in our ability to uplift each other, to create a sanctuary where everyone feels valued and heard.

By embracing this model of communal empowerment, we foster an environment where others can share their fears and dreams. Just as Esther found her courage fueled by the communal cries for justice, we too can discover the power that lies in solidarity. Any act of bravery becomes magnified when it is supported by a community poised for action. Each courageous voice adds to the resounding call for justice, for healing, and for change.

In the aftermath of crises, the task of rebuilding often falls heavier on individual shoulders. However, by remembering how Esther's decisions spurred her people into action, we recognize that we do not need to navigate these waters alone. Esther's legacy is one of collaboration; it teaches us that when one among us rises, they inspire others to do the same. Furthermore, it is essential to understand that communal empowerment is a two-way street. Just as Esther benefited from her community, she also served as a catalyst for their empowerment. Her bravery inspired her people to stand together and act in unison. Communities around us need individuals who are willing to step forward, to become voices for the voiceless, and to bear the weight of injustice. In a time when Esther's people felt vulnerable, she became a source of strength, illuminating the path toward hope. This transformation can inspire us to seek out ways to be advocates within our communities, whether that means lending a listening ear, providing support in times of need, or standing up for those who cannot stand for themselves. Each act of kindness we extend can create ripples of courage that resonate throughout our circles. Like Esther, we can recognize that our choices hold power not only for ourselves but for others as well.

As we continue to explore Esther's journey, it is crucial to acknowledge the role that faith can play in communal empowerment. Esther's decision to pray and fast with her community wasn't merely a ritual; it was an act of solidarity that fostered a deeper connection with both God and her people. Faith can be a unifying force, bringing individuals together to work toward a common goal. In moments of uncertainty, lean on the shared beliefs and values of those around you to find strength and direction.

Esther's resilience and wisdom serve as a powerful reminder that true courage is born from community. As the story unfolds, we see how her bravery not only saved her life but also safeguarded her nation. There is a profound lesson in recognizing that heroism does not exist in isolation. Rather, it breathes and thrives in the atmosphere of support, understanding, and collective resolve.

Let us ponder the invitation to participate actively in our communities, to foster environments where courage is celebrated and nurtured. It is not solely about facing crises; it is about transforming our networks into vibrant entities where each member plays a vital role. By uplifting the voices of those around us, we create a sanctuary of empowerment where every individual is encouraged to rise.

In conclusion, as we examine the theme of communal empowerment illuminated by Esther's story, we see the multifaceted dimensions that elevate individual acts of courage to extraordinary heights. Esther's bravery, combined with the unwavering support of her community, provides a powerful paradigm for examining our roles today. The tapestry of life is rich with opportunities to connect, uplift, and transform our shared experiences into collective resilience. In a world often marked by division and isolation, let us draw inspiration from Esther's legacy. May we be emboldened to embrace our communities, recognizing that our individual strength is magnified when shared. Together, we can be the voices that echo courage, compassion, and hope, ensuring that in every crisis, community will rise and empower its members to overcome. As we reflect on our own lives, let us ask how we can contribute to the betterment of those around us, thus writing our own chapters of courage within the larger story of humanity. This is the essence of communal empowerment, and it is a journey worth undertaking together.

FORGIVENESS AND REDEMPTION: BREAKING THE CHAINS

The Path to Forgiveness

Forgiveness is a monumental endeavor, an act that transcends mere words and actions. Throughout the narratives of the Bible, various figures demonstrate the power of forgiveness, both the act of extending it and the incredible freedom found in receiving it. Their stories unfold in rich layers, revealing the trials and triumphs that accompany the journey toward reconciliation. As we navigate through these biblical accounts, we can unearth profound lessons that challenge us to consider our paths toward forgiveness in our own lives.

One of the most poignant stories of forgiveness is that of Joseph. Betrayed by his brothers, sold into slavery, and wrongfully imprisoned, Joseph endured unimaginable suffering. The emotional wounds inflicted by those who were supposed to love him ran deep. Yet, when he ultimately rose to power in Egypt and faced his brothers again, he did not seek revenge. Instead, Joseph recognized the greater purpose behind his suffering. In Genesis 50:20, he tells them, "You intended to harm me, but God intended it for good to accomplish what is now being done, the saving of many lives." Joseph's ability to forgive stemmed not just from a desire for personal peace but from a profound understanding of divine providence. His journey illustrates that forgiveness can lead to healing not just for oneself but for a community at large.

Like Joseph, Hannah also encountered deep personal anguish, grappling with her own unanswered prayers and social stigma. Her story, centered on longing and desperation for a child, reveals another facet of how our struggles can lead us to forgiveness. Hannah's prayers were filled with raw emotion, and the contrast of her suffering against the taunts of Peninnah, her rival, left her feeling isolated. Yet, instead of harboring bitterness, Hannah remained steadfast in her faith, pouring out her heart to God. Her eventual joy upon receiving Samuel, her promised son, led her to surrender her long-held desire to God, embodying true forgiveness in the process. She gave Samuel back to God, saying, "For this child I prayed, and the Lord has granted me my petition that I made to him" (1 Samuel 1:27). Hannah's story teaches us that forgiveness often requires us to release our deepest desires, entrusting them to a power greater than ourselves.

The New Testament offers another profound perspective on forgiveness through the parable of the prodigal son. This narrative encapsulates the essence of redemption and reconciliation. The father's unwillingness to hold a grudge against his wayward son illustrates unconditional love and an open heart ready to forgive. When the son returns home, remorseful and humbled, the father does not berate him but rather embraces him with open arms, celebrating his return. This powerful imagery reflects our own struggles with forgiveness, both forgiving others and receiving forgiveness ourselves. Often, the hardest person to forgive is ourselves, and the father's example encourages us to let go of guilt and shame, recognizing that forgiveness is an essential part of growth.

Jesus, in His ministry, continually emphasized the significance of forgiveness. He taught His followers to forgive not just once but countless times, embodying a radical understanding of grace. In Matthew 18:21-22, Peter asks Jesus how many times he should forgive someone who sins against him. Jesus responds, "I tell you, not seven times, but seventy-seven times." This passage suggests that forgiveness should have no limits. It's not merely a technique to resolve conflict but rather a posture of the heart, a willingness to let go of resentment and bitterness. Jesus exemplifies this in His final moments on the cross, where He prayed for those who crucified Him, saying, "Father, forgive them, for they do not know what they are doing" (Luke 23:34). His ability to forgive even in the face of unimaginable pain demonstrates the transformative power of love.

Moses provides another captivating narrative related to forgiveness and reconciliation. The account of the Israelites during their wanderings through the desert showcases how grievances can escalate into strongholds of bitterness. As Moses leads them, they often grumble against him, blaming him for their hardships. However, he continually intercedes with God on their behalf, showing grace and humility. Moses' willingness to forgive helps maintain unity within the community, highlighting that forgiveness is not just about personal feelings but also about communal harmony. His story teaches us that true leadership involves the capacity to forgive and foster reconciliation within groups.

As we reflect on these biblical figures and their journeys, we find common threads that weave through their stories – struggles, pain, resilience, and ultimately, the journey toward forgiveness. These narratives urge us to examine our own hearts and recognize the chains that bind us when we struggle to forgive. The act of holding onto grudges or past hurts is ultimately self-destructive, preventing us from experiencing the full richness of life that God intends for us. Forgiveness has the power to break these chains, offering a pathway toward healing and wholeness.

For many, the journey toward forgiveness begins with acknowledging the depth of hurt experienced. The road may be filled with anger, confusion, and fear. It is essential to confront these emotions rather than suppress them. Hannah's story reminds us that it's okay to express our pain, whether through fervent prayer or honest conversations with ourselves and trusted loved ones. By bringing our emotions into the light, we can begin to see them from a different perspective, one that allows for healing.

Consider the power of perspective as illustrated in the story of Naomi and Ruth. After enduring profound loss and hardship, Naomi struggled with bitterness, feeling as though God had dealt harshly with her. Yet Ruth, her daughter-in-law, chose to stand by Naomi in her darkest moments, embodying steadfast love and loyalty. Ruth's commitment to Naomi reflects that forgiveness can flourish in the embrace of support and solidarity.

Through their relationship, both women experienced a transformation – Naomi found hope once again, and Ruth was rewarded for her faithfulness.

Forgiveness does not imply forgetting or minimizing the offense; rather, it allows us to move beyond the pain and reclaim our lives. This process can take time and may require the gentle guidance of the Holy Spirit. Engaging with scripture through prayer and reflection can illuminate paths forward, empowering us to forgive those who have hurt us, as well as ourselves for past mistakes. Moreover, engaging in community can play a significant role in the healing process. Just as the early church provided support and fellowship, sharing our stories of hurt and forgiveness in a trusted environment can facilitate a release from the burdens we carry. Hannah's annual pilgrimage to Shiloh was not simply a personal journey; it encompassed a communal experience of faith and vulnerability. Ultimately, it is within a community of faith that we can find encouragement and strength to let go.

One key aspect of cultivating a forgiving heart is understanding the difference between justice and revenge. The biblical narrative repeatedly teaches us that vengeance is the Lord's domain. When we feel wronged, it is tempting to seek retribution, believing it may provide solace. However, this desire can lead us down a path of bitterness and sorrow. Instead, we are invited to trust that God sees our pain and will ultimately bring justice in His timing. Joseph's example serves as a powerful reminder that he left vengeance to God, choosing instead to offer grace and love.

As we explore forgiveness, it is vital to address the issue of self-forgiveness. Many individuals struggle with the weight of past mistakes and failures. The narratives of the Bible are replete with characters who stumble and fall yet find redemption and purpose in their lives. For instance, Peter's denial of Jesus marks a moment of profound failure. Yet after the resurrection, Jesus foregoes condemnation, instead asking Peter, "Do you love me?" (John 21:15). This moment of restoration was not just a display of forgiveness but an invitation for Peter to step into his purpose once more. Our struggles with self-forgiveness often mirror Peter's journey, showing us that our failures do not disqualify us from God's love. In fact, they can be the stepping stones toward our calling.

The process of forgiveness also involves letting go of expectations surrounding the behavior of others. Often, we attach conditions to our forgiveness, expecting the other party to acknowledge their wrongdoing or to demonstrate remorse. However, our ability to forgive should not depend on others' actions or attitudes. Instead, we are called to extend grace, releasing ourselves from the burden of resentment. The widow's willingness to forgive her debts, as paralleled in the teachings of Jesus, reminds us that forgiveness is a gift we give ourselves rather than a transaction we negotiate with others.

Lastly, the journey toward forgiveness culminates in the hope of redemption. Forgiveness is not simply an act of the present but unlocks pathways for renewed relationships and future possibilities. When we choose to forgive, we position ourselves and others to experience transformative grace, a chance to start anew. In every biblical account, each act of forgiveness paved the way for healing, restoration, and a deeper relationship with God and one another. By extending forgiveness, we participate in a divine cycle of grace, allowing God to work through our lives and impact those around us.

As we navigate our own paths toward forgiveness, we must remember that the journey is seldom straightforward. It can involve setbacks, heartache, and moments of doubt. Yet, as Hannah's story demonstrates, surrendering our struggles to God, reminiscent of the biblical figures, enables us to rediscover the transformative power of forgiveness. Embracing this journey requires faith and the courage to embrace our own vulnerabilities, but it ultimately leads us toward wholeness, a gift that only forgiveness can bestow.

In conclusion, "The Path to Forgiveness" is both personal and communal. The biblical stories of Joseph, Hannah, the Prodigal Son, Moses, and others offer profound illustrations of how forgiveness weaves through our lives and often leads us to reconnection and renewal. As we reflect on their journeys, we are encouraged to examine our hearts, confront our pain, and cultivate a forgiving spirit, a blessing that ultimately breaks our chains and propels us toward a life defined by grace and redemption. Each step on this journey, while challenging, is one that draws us closer to the abundant life that God desires for each of us. Let us move forward, inspired by these narratives, ready to embark on our own paths toward forgiveness, embracing the fullness of life that awaits us.

The Healing Power of Redemption

Forgiveness and redemption are two of the most profound themes woven throughout the tapestry of the Bible. They resonate in the stories of the faithful, echoing the cries of the lost and the weary, and offering a path toward healing and transformation. As we delve into the healing power of redemption, we turn to Hannah's poignant story, a narrative that serves as an anchor for our exploration.

Hannah, a woman of deep faith, embodies the struggle of many: the longing for a child when that desire seems unattainable. Yet, her tale is not only about longing but also about the painful experience of barrenness, the weight of societal expectations, and the heartache of rivalry. In her journey, we witness the intertwining of forgiveness and redemption, both her own and that of others around her. This subchapter seeks to unearth the rich layers of redemption woven into her life and extend those themes into the broader narrative of the Bible.

Hannah's story is set in a world where women were often defined by their ability to bear children. In her case, the deep pain of infertility was compounded by her husband's other wife, Peninnah, who relentlessly taunted her for her inability to conceive. This created an environment laden with bitterness, jealousy, and sorrow. Yet, it is from this tumultuous place that the seeds of redemption began to sprout. In her anguish, Hannah chose to turn to the Lord in prayer, pouring out her heart at the temple in Shiloh. This act of vulnerability is critical for understanding the healing power of redemption. Hannah laid bare her deepest pain before God, which represents the first step in the journey toward both forgiveness and redemption. The act of confession, of unveiling our struggles, can open the door to healing. In the Bible, many characters, much like Hannah, confronted their pain openly, allowing God to intercede and reshape their narratives. This sets a precedent for us: to acknowledge our hurt can catalyze profound change.

For Hannah, the pivotal moment came when Eli, the priest, saw her deep sorrow and spoke words of blessing over her. In this encounter, we witness how important it is for others to be instruments of God's grace. Redemption is not merely a solitary journey; it often involves the community of faith in our experiences of forgiveness and healing. In Hannah's case, Eli's recognition and blessing acted as a catalyst for her transformation. She went from a place of bitterness and despair to one of hope and assurance. This transformation underlines the powerful effect that compassion and understanding can have on those who are hurting.

Hannah returned home, her heart lightened, and soon after, she conceived and bore a son named Samuel. His name means "God has heard." This gift was not merely the culmination of her deepest desire; it was a manifestation of God's redemptive power. In giving birth to Samuel, Hannah experienced not just the joy of motherhood but also the deeper reality of being a part of God's unfolding plan. This reflects the essence of biblical redemption: God uses our brokenness, our longing, and our pain to create something beautiful and transformative.

As we traverse the broader biblical landscape, redemption appears as an unwavering thread. The story of the Israelites' exodus from Egypt serves as a poignant reflection of this theme. Just as Hannah was released from the bonds of her despair, the Israelites were liberated from the chains of slavery. This grand narrative is marked by God's unwavering commitment to His people, extending forgiveness and a promise of future hope. At the crux lies a profound understanding: to embrace God's redemptive love, one must first acknowledge the need for forgiveness. The Israelites needed to recognize their own failures and turn back to God before they could receive liberation.

The Psalms, often born from places of pain and longing, echo this redemptive thread. David, in his lamentations, continually seeks God's forgiveness. Psalm 51 is a prime example, where David cries out for mercy, seeking restoration after his sin. Here, we see that redemption is not just about the act of being forgiven but also about the transformation that follows when one decides to redefine their relationship with God. David's heartfelt cry is a mirror to Hannah's prayer – both embody the essence of turning our sorrow into worship. In their vulnerabilities, both women and men find the strength to rise redeemed.

This theme crescendos within the New Testament, where redemption is embodied in Christ. Through His sacrifice, the ultimate act of forgiveness is extended to all of humanity, showcasing that healing is intricately bound up with the mercy of God. Jesus' teachings encourage the practice of forgiveness among one another, emphasizing that forgiveness is not merely a theological concept but a personal and community-building act. Just like Hannah's act of sincere prayer led to her transformation, forgiveness leads to reconciliation and wholeness.

Forgiveness is the bridge toward healing. However, it is necessary to acknowledge the challenges that come with it. The act of forgiving does not negate the pain or the gravity of the offense; rather, it offers a pathway toward healing. Hannah, too, had to confront her past. Even after she bore Samuel, she committed him to the Lord's service. This act encapsulates both a response to her redemption and a step toward healing the wounds of her earlier suffering. She did not harbor resentment toward Peninnah, despite the years of ridicule. By focusing on her covenant with the Lord, Hannah's transformation illustrates that forgiveness often begins when we choose to align our hearts with God's purpose. Her story reminds us that redemption is an active process. It requires stepping away from the hurt and choosing to embrace a new identity rooted in hope.

In our journey toward embracing forgiveness, we must also confront the reality of our personal narratives. Women across the Bible – like Rahab, Ruth, and Mary – exemplify lives marked by redemption. Rahab, the harlot of Jericho, displayed faith that overcame her past, earning her a place in Christ's lineage. Ruth, a Moabite widow, transformed her grief into steadfast loyalty and love, ultimately leading to her own redemption in a new world. Mary, the mother of Jesus, carried the immense weight of her pregnancy in a society that often defined women by their circumstances. Their stories converge on the principle that redemption is not confined to a single moment; it flourishes when embraced as a lifelong journey.

Healing from pain, suffering, and betrayal demands grace, both from the Divine and through our relationships with others. Consider the women in the Bible who exemplified forgiveness; each story echoes Hannah's in its depth of struggle and eventual transformation. These narratives collectively underscore that forgiveness, while at times arduous, lays the groundwork for healing and redemption.

Reflecting on our lives, perhaps we have lived through experiences that felt unending, full of despair, taunts, or failures. Like Hannah, we may have found solace in prayer, yet subsequently found ourselves wrestling with feelings of inadequacy or resentment. This journey toward redemption often reveals the truth that forgiveness is less about the one who wronged us and more about freeing ourselves from the chains that bind our hearts.

In a profound sense, Hannah's story echoes our struggles with feelings of worthiness shaped by society and circumstance. Today, many face similar battles in their homes, workplaces, and communities. Hannah's voice rises above the abyss of despair, reminding us of the necessity of nurturing our spirits through connection with God and others. In times of brokenness, leaning into a community reminds us that we are not alone, and healing flourishes within the embrace of shared faith and understanding.

To cultivate a spirit of redemption, we must practice forgiveness, first by acknowledging our failings and then by extending grace to those who have wronged us. This cycle of forgiveness and healing mirrors Hannah's own odyssey. She emerged from her pain not only renewed by her prayers and blessings but transformed into a vessel of worship and dedication to God, ultimately redirecting her life and heart toward faith and service.

In conclusion, we reflect on the profound healing power of redemption depicted through Hannah's life and intertwined with the greater biblical narrative. Her story reminds us that forgiveness leads to healing, a healing not merely limited to our wounds but expansive enough to reshape communities and histories. As we absorb these lessons, may we carry forward the practice of forgiveness as a daily act of grace, allowing the power of redemption to transform our own lives and those around us, turning past pains into testimonies of hope and healing. Just as Hannah dedicated her son to the Lord, let us also offer our stories of redemption back to God as a testament to His unfailing love and grace. By doing so, we join in the rich tapestry of women of faith, becoming part of a larger story that speaks to the power of forgiveness and the profound beauty of redemption. Through every tear shed in sorrow, may we rise in renewed faith, knowing that in Christ, all things are made new.

Finding Freedom

In the journey of life, the weight of unaddressed hurts can often feel unbearable. We carry these grievances with us, letting them shape our thoughts, mold our actions, and cloud our relationships. The burden of unforgiveness can be so heavy that it prevents us from moving forward, trapping us in a cycle of resentment and pain. This is a truth woven into the fabric of many women's stories found in the Bible, and it is particularly evident in the life of Hannah.

Hannah, a woman marked by her experiences of heartache and longing, found herself entangled in a web of bitterness and despair. Praying for the child she so desperately wanted, she dealt with the scorn of Peninnah, her husband's other wife, who taunted her endlessly. In her anguish, Hannah faced a choice, a choice that many of us face when wronged: to hold on or to let go. Her journey illustrates the liberating nature of forgiveness and how letting go can lead to personal freedom and reconciliation.

Forgiveness is often misconstrued as an act of weakness. It can feel akin to losing a battle, as if we are giving our pain the power to dictate our feelings. But in reality, forgiveness is a courageous and powerful choice, one that opens the door to liberation. It is not about forgetting the wrongs done to us or minimizing the hurt; rather, it is about recognizing the pain and consciously deciding to release its grip over our lives. Hannah's act of pouring out her heart to God in the temple serves as an example of this deliberate release. In her prayer, she not only expressed her sorrow but also released her burden into God's hands. This pivotal moment marked the beginning of her liberation.

The act of forgiving ourselves and others creates an opportunity for healing. The chains of guilt, shame, and anger dissolve when we decide to break free from the mindset that keeps us bound to our pain. Hannah's story reminds us that although the journey to forgiveness may be challenging, it is also transformative. Through her vulnerability before God, she was able to experience a profound sense of peace, which is often the first taste of freedom that many seek.

Furthermore, recognizing the commonality of our struggles can be a source of comfort and encouragement. Hannah's pain was not isolated; she shared it with so many other women throughout scripture and throughout history. Women like Miriam, who faced her own trials bravely, and Esther, who stood courageously for her people, remind us that we are not alone. They faced adversity with grit and determination, and their stories echo the strength found in vulnerability.

To understand the depth of forgiveness, we must also grapple with our perceptions of justice and retribution. In a world that often equates wrongdoing with punishment, we might struggle with the notion of letting go. However, forgiveness does not negate justice; it simply redefines it. In Hannah's prayer, she not only sought relief from her sorrow but also placed her trust in God's ultimate judgment. By surrendering her pain, she positioned herself for divine intervention, a powerful reminder that in relinquishing our need for control, we open ourselves up to possibilities beyond our understanding.

The release of burdens is not merely an act of personal emancipation but an invitation to reconciliation. Relationships, whether familial, platonic, or romantic, can often become strained by unresolved conflicts. The path to healing often begins with a dialogue rooted in forgiveness. Hannah's relationship with her husband, Elkanah, is pivotal in understanding this aspect of her journey. Despite the presence of Peninnah and her jibes, Hannah was able to maintain a bond with Elkanah that was based on love and understanding. Their interactions, laced with mutual respect, emphasize that healing and forgiveness create space for deeper connections.

It is intriguing to see how forgiveness can reach beyond our immediate relationships and extend to broader communities. When women forgive and support one another, they form networks of strength that can lead to collective healing. Hannah's story does not end with her personal victory; its ripples affect those around her, culminating in a legacy of hope for future generations. The act of forgiveness paves the way for deeper interconnections and creates an environment of mercy and compassion.

As we delve into the act of forgiving, we cannot overlook the importance of allowing ourselves the grace to heal over time. Forgiveness is not a singular event but a journey, a continuous process of releasing the hold that past grievances have over us. Just like Hannah, who faced her pain repeatedly before fully embracing her freedom, we too must be patient with ourselves. Healing begins the moment we make the choice to forgive, but it does not mean that the road ahead will be easy or linear.

Practical steps toward forgiveness involve acknowledging our pain, allowing ourselves to feel it, and seeking guidance, whether through prayer, community support, or professional help. By creating avenues to process our feelings constructively, we can dismantle the walls built by hurt. Hannah's commitment to prayer is a powerful example of this practice. It serves as a reminder of the transformative power of seeking divine assistance in our struggles.

Communities of faith are especially crucial in facilitating the process of forgiveness. They can serve as safe spaces where women share their stories, find understanding, and extend grace to one another. In these circles, we discover that forgiveness is not an isolated act but a collective movement toward healing. When women in biblical times gathered to support one another, they created a culture of resilience that echoes through the ages. Whether through prayer circles, study groups, or informal gatherings, the act of collective forgiveness cultivates an atmosphere of love and support.

In our lives today, this could manifest in various ways. Perhaps it is having a difficult conversation with a loved one where both parties acknowledge their failings. Maybe it involves participating in a community service project that embodies the principles of forgiveness and reconciliation. Each step we take toward forgiveness is akin to a brick laid on the path to freedom, leading us away from bitterness and toward peace.

Ultimately, freedom through forgiveness not only liberates the soul but also instills hope. Hannah's story culminates in her answered prayer when she is finally blessed with a child. However, the hope that blooms from forgiveness is far more profound than the fulfillment of a desire. It is an overarching hope that nourishes our spirits, reminds us that we are not defined by our past, and assures us that healing is always possible. Reflecting on this hope can bring light to the darkest corners of our lives. When we have released the weight of unforgiveness, we gain clarity that allows us to pursue our dreams and passions with renewed vigor. Just as Hannah, after her prayer, was freed to embrace her role as a mother, we too find ourselves empowered to step into our destinies when we actively choose to let go of the chains that bind us.

Embracing forgiveness is not an easy endeavor, but it is one that sets us upon a liberated path, a path underscored by grace, mercy, and healing. Our stories may not mirror Hannah's in every detail; perhaps we grapple with different forms of hurt, unresolved conflicts, or missed opportunities. Yet, the underlying principles remain the same: through seeking forgiveness, embracing healing, and nurturing hope, we can break the chains that hinder our growth.

As this narrative draws to a close, remember that forgiveness is an ongoing journey. Reflect on the burdens you carry and consider the power of releasing them. Embrace the liberating nature of forgiveness as a means to cultivate deeper connections with others and ultimately foster a relationship with yourself rooted in grace. In choosing forgiveness, you make a profound declaration, not only to the world around you but also to your own spirit: I am free.

With this freedom comes the opportunity to write your own story, just as Hannah did, one where hope reigns and burdens are transformed into blessings. Through each act of forgiveness and every step toward reconciliation, we emerge not only as survivors of our pasts but as women endowed with the strength to shape our narratives moving forward. Let us embrace this gift and share it within our spheres, creating a legacy of healing and hope that resonates for generations to come. In doing so, we honor the stories of those who have come before us and pave a hopeful path for those who will follow. Forgiveness is our key to freedom; let it unlock the doors of our potential, inviting us to step boldly into the future.

VOICES OF THE WOMEN: GATHERING THREADS OF LEGACY

Tapestry of Stories

In thinking about the stories of women in the Bible, one cannot help but visualize a beautifully intricate tapestry woven from countless threads. Each thread represents an individual experience, rich with its own colors and textures, together forming a larger picture that is both complex and compelling. The lives of these women intertwine and intersect at various points, revealing a legacy of strength, resilience, faith, and courage. Their stories invite us to explore not only the distinctiveness of each woman's journey but also the collective narratives that emerge when we consider their lives in tandem.

Hannah's story, as the anchor of this exploration, epitomizes the struggles and triumphs of women seeking fulfillment in a patriarchal society. Her heartfelt cries for a child resonate with the profound desires and hopes many women continue to experience. In her deep anguish, we find a thread that runs through the lives of others, those who long for something desperately, whether it be love, acceptance, recognition, or purpose. Yet, the revelations from their stories illuminate the idea that such desires, though personal, are rarely isolated. As we dive into the lives of Naomi, Ruth, Leah, Deborah, and other biblical figures, we reveal the interconnected nature of their experiences, each one contributing to a grander narrative of faith and perseverance.

Naomi stands as a testament to the power of loss and redemption. Her story is not solely one of grief but one of transformation and loyalty. Having lost her husband and sons, Naomi chooses to return to Bethlehem, the land of her roots, embracing the bitterness of her journey yet finding unexpected grace in her daughter-in-law, Ruth. Their bond forms another thread in the tapestry, a tale of commitment that transcends cultural and familial boundaries. Ruth's steadfastness embodies the loyalty that enriches our understanding of kinship and support in times of adversity. Ruth's declaration to Naomi, "Where you go, I will go; where you stay, I will stay," reverberates through generations, illustrating that true love is often found in commitment during our darkest hours.

Leah, often overshadowed by her more beloved sister Rachel, becomes a narrative of longing for love and acknowledgment. Her story urges us to examine the complexities of jealousy, acceptance, and identity. In a world where her worth is measured against her sister's beauty and charm, Leah's journey unfolds with deep emotional layers. The names she gives to her children signal her inner struggles and aspirations. With each son born, she cries out for recognition and love, a reminder of the universal quest for self-worth. Leah's story compels us to reflect on the significance of finding value within ourselves, regardless of how others perceive us or the love we receive.

Deborah shines as a beacon of female leadership in a time when women's voices were often silenced. As a prophetess, she exemplifies wisdom and courage, leading Israel in a time of great uncertainty. Her story invites us to embrace the strength of our convictions, encouraging women not only to share their voices but to step into roles of leadership and guidance. Deborah calls Barak to rally an army against Sisera, displaying her confidence in God's direction and ultimate victory. The tapestry is enriched by her indomitable spirit, showing us how following one's calling can inspire entire communities to act and reclaim their destinies.

Each of these women's narratives contributes to a grander theme of intertwining stories. Together, they emphasize the richness of women's experiences throughout biblical history. Their various backgrounds, struggles, and victories highlight the importance of solidarity, showing how, through shared experiences, one can find comfort and wisdom in the company of others. The lessons gleaned from Hannah, Naomi, Ruth, Leah, and Deborah reveal that while their paths may differ, the threads of hope and resilience bind them together. As we explore these stories, we see the common threads of despair and hope, struggle and triumph, woven into the very fabric of their lives. Each woman, in her unique way, faces challenges that reflect broader truths about the human condition. The feelings of longing, loneliness, love, and legacy reverberate throughout time, establishing a profound connection not only amongst themselves but with us as well.

The tapestry of stories calls us to ask poignant questions about our own lives. What do we desire? How do we overcome life's trials? Just as Hannah poured out her heart in prayer, we are encouraged to voice our deepest longings. Naomi teaches us that even when faced with despair, returning to one's roots can birth hope anew. With Ruth, we learn the power of loyalty and the significance of standing by one another. Leah reminds us of the importance of self-acceptance amidst comparison, while Deborah encourages us to take charge and seize leadership roles, regardless of societal constraints.

Throughout history, women have navigated layers of complexity, woven their narratives, and faced challenges that shaped their identities. In examining their stories through the lens of a tapestry, we come to appreciate the intricate nature of these experiences. Each woman adds her thread to the vast fabric, encapsulating emotions and challenges that resonate even today.

The tapestry is not simply a relic of the past; it serves as a mirror reflecting our own journeys. Every woman who reads these biblical stories can see herself in Hannah's grief, Naomi's resilience, Ruth's loyalty, Leah's struggle for recognition, and Deborah's courage. Each of us carries our threads, some bright and colorful, others frayed and faded. But together, they create a distinctive narrative that defines who we are and how we navigate our own lives.

As we delve deeper into the experiences of these women, we invite the readers to stitch their own threads into this rich tapestry. What lessons have you learned from your struggles? How have your connections with other women altered the course of your journey? In sharing these stories, we honor the legacy of those who came before us while forging our unique paths. Just as the women of the Bible inspire us, we, too, have the potential to impact others, weaving a legacy that echoes through time.

In contemplating the diverse experiences within this grand tapestry, we foster connection. By recognizing the interconnectedness of our stories, we dismantle the complexities of isolation and competition that can arise in our journeys. Instead, we celebrate the joy of sisterhood and the power of solidarity, reaffirming that together, we can weave a narrative that is compelling and transformative.

The women in the Bible are not mere historical figures; they are vessels of wisdom whose experiences resonate across the ages. Each thread of their lives contributes to a collective legacy, encouraging us to draw strength from their stories and apply the lessons learned to our present-day lives. Through Hannah's anguished prayer, Naomi's resilient spirit, Ruth's unwavering loyalty, Leah's quest for love, and Deborah's courageous leadership, we come to understand that our stories, too, are part of a larger tapestry, one that continues to be woven with each new generation.

As we conclude this subchapter, let us carry the threads of these women's legacies into our lives. In moments of sorrow, let us remember Hannah's cries. In times of uncertainty, look to Naomi for strength. When seeking companionship, model Ruth's loyalty. In our struggles for acknowledgment, find confidence in Leah's identity. And when called to lead, embrace Deborah's courage.

The tapestry of stories is not only the legacy of those biblical women; it is a call to action for us all. As we gather the threads of our own narratives, let us celebrate the interconnectedness of our journeys, weaving together a legacy that honors those who have come before us and paves the way for those yet to come. Together, let us continue to create a beautiful tapestry of stories that reflects our resilience, strength, and shared humanity.

Lessons Through Time

In the tapestry of scripture, the narratives of biblical women are woven with profound lessons that transcend the boundaries of time and culture. Their stories are not merely relics of a distant past but resonate deeply in the complexities of our modern lives. As we explore the voices of these remarkable women, it becomes evident that the wisdom they impart holds significance for each of us today. Through their struggles, triumphs, faith, and resilience, they offer insights that continue to inspire and challenge, beckoning us to actively engage with these enduring lessons in our everyday lives.

Take Hannah, for instance – her heart-wrenching journey of yearning and devotion illuminates the power of prayer and the depths of hope. In a society that often overlooks the quiet anguish of the marginalized, Hannah's story speaks to those who grapple with feelings of inadequacy and desire. Her poignant cries for a child echo through the ages, reminding us that longing is a universal experience. As women today navigate the pressures of parenthood, career ambitions, and personal aspirations, Hannah stands as a beacon of unwavering faith. Her tenacity in the face of despair encourages us to pour our hearts out in genuine prayer, to voice our deepest desires and fears, knowing that we are heard.

Hannah's experience in the temple, where she poured out her soul before God, illustrates a radical authenticity that many modern women find liberating. In a world saturated with curated images of perfection, the rawness of her vulnerability invites us to shed the masks we often wear. It is through this lens of honesty that we can engage with our struggles – be they relational, professional, or spiritual – recognizing that it is acceptable to bring our brokenness to God. In a society that often champions self-sufficiency, Hannah's story teaches us the importance of surrender and reliance on a higher power, prompting us to seek out spiritual communities where we can share our stories and support one another.

Across the pages of Scripture, we encounter other women who reinforce these lessons and broaden our understanding of strength, resilience, and faith. Consider the cunning and bravery of Jael, who took decisive action in a time of oppression, embodying the essence of courage. Her story implores us to recognize that action taken in the face of injustice can lead to transformative change. In our contemporary context, women are asked to step into roles of leadership and advocacy, fighting against inequality and standing up for both themselves and others. Jael's legacy encourages us to take bold steps, whether in our workplaces, communities, or households, reminding us that we are capable of effecting significant change when we respond compassionately and courageously to the needs around us.

Similarly, Ruth's unwavering loyalty and resilience continue to echo through generations. Her commitment to Naomi challenges us to cultivate relationships that are deeply rooted in support and sacrifice. In an age where individualism often reigns supreme, Ruth's story acts as a powerful reminder of the value of community and familial bonds. It prompts us to reevaluate our commitments to those around us, urging us to stand by one another through adversity. We learn from Ruth that love often comes with sacrifice but yields rich rewards, a message that resonates with both the joys and challenges of contemporary relationships.

Esther's journey opens another dimension of the discussion surrounding legacy, the interplay between personal agency and collective responsibility. Her courageous decision to step forward as an advocate for her people resonates deeply, especially in a world that requires women to find their voices in the face of oppression. Esther's story brings to light the necessity of using our platform, however small or large, to advocate for justice, challenging us to reflect on our roles in our families and communities. The legacy of Esther teaches us that even in moments of fear and uncertainty, courage can lead to life-altering outcomes, encouraging us to embrace moments where we must stand up for what is right.

The lessons from these women intertwine, each thread contributing to a greater narrative of resilience and agency. As we look to the stories of these biblical women, we realize they are not just figures in ancient history but are representatives of the myriad experiences women face today. Each lesson encourages us to actively engage with our faith, our relationships, and our mission in the world. The timeless nature of these lessons invites us to see ourselves in their stories, serving as mirror reflections of our struggles and victories.

In reflecting on these narratives, we discover that they challenge us to confront our own biases and limitations. Their stories prompt us to question how we perceive our current challenges, whether they are seasonal trials such as grief, betrayal, or personal failures. In many ways, these biblical women provide companionship for our own journeys. As we struggle with our own identities, ambitions, and choices, they show us that doubt and struggle don't diminish our worth; they enhance our stories.

Engaging with these legacies involves both personal introspection and collective action. It means taking time to reflect on how the courage of Esther can embolden us to advocate for social justice in our communities or how Hannah's example encourages us to cultivate a life steeped in prayer and trust. There are also lessons in surrender and vulnerability, an encouragement to share our stories honestly and allow our sisters to uplift us through their own. The communal aspect of learning and growing in faith has never been more vital as we navigate the complexities of modern living together.

As we gather these threads of legacy, it becomes clear that the stories of these women are not merely ancient tales meant to inspire. They are blueprints for a life lived in courage and faith. They remind us to honor our emotional truths while seeking out the divine, just as Hannah did in the temple. They prompt us to speak life over one another as Ruth spoke to Naomi and to take action when we see injustice, as Jael did in her courageous moment. They implore us to recognize the strength we hold in advocating for ourselves and our community, just as Esther did with her people.

Perhaps the most profound lesson lies in understanding the importance of sharing these stories with one another. As we recount the experiences of Hannah, Esther, Ruth, and Jael within our own circles, we create a legacy of our own, one that encourages the next generation of women to rise, to voice their struggles, and to act with confidence. In today's landscape of often isolating pressures, sharing our journeys fosters connection and resilience. We empower one another to embrace our stories fully, allowing these lessons to take root in our lives.

In doing so, we create a culture where these biblical women's legacies are not just read but lived, breathed, and celebrated. We begin to see social gatherings not just as opportunities for casual conversation but as platforms for sharing wisdom and encouragement. We bring these narratives into our meetings, our homes, and our hearts. We allow Hannah's prayers to inspire honesty in our discussions about motherhood, career aspirations, and spiritual growth. We let Esther's courage guide us as we confront the injustices we see in our daily lives. The transformative power of these lessons lies not merely in our understanding of them but in the act of applying them, turning ancient wisdom into contemporary action.

Thus, as we navigate through the struggles and victories of life, let us remember the timeless legacies of these biblical women. Let us carry their stories with us as we endeavor to build a community of support, love, and resilience. The powerful echoes of Hannah, Ruth, Esther, Jael, and the many others remind us to embrace our journeys and use our voices boldly. With each shared experience, we continue to weave a tapestry of faith, strength, and love, creating a legacy that will endure for generations to come. Though their stories were etched in the annals of time, the lessons learned remain vibrant and relevant, waiting to be embraced and activated in our lives today. The call to action is clear: let us learn, share, and live out the essence of these incredible women, crafting a narrative that honors their legacies while brave enough to step into our own.

Inspiring Future Generations

In the quiet spaces between the stories we tell, there lingers a vibrant tapestry woven not just from the threads of our experiences but also from the lessons learned by generations before us. The stories of women in the Bible – Hannah, Miriam, Ruth, Esther – are not just ancient accounts; they are living narratives that pulse with relevance even today. Each woman's journey holds profound insights into faith, resilience, courage, and the intimate relationship we share with the Divine. As we draw to a close the collective lessons offered by these figures, it becomes imperative to consider our role in this continuity of wisdom.

Life is a story, and every life has the potential to inspire. With each decision we make, with each challenge we face, we add another line to our unique narratives, impacting not just our own lives but also the lives of those who will follow in our footprints. The notion of legacy is not merely about what we leave behind in material terms; it is fundamentally about the stories we share, the lessons we impart, and the values we embody. It is through this lens of legacy that we will explore our capacity to inspire future generations, reflecting particularly on the shared wisdom from women in Scripture.

Beginning with Hannah, her story is one of heartache transformed into hope. She was a woman who faced despair amid societal expectations, yet through her fervent prayers and unwavering faith, she became the mother of Samuel, a pivotal figure in Israel's history. Hannah's legacy extends beyond her immediate circumstances; it encompasses the notion of dedicating oneself fully to God's will, demonstrating the power of both personal sacrifice and divine purpose. Her willingness to offer Samuel back to God reflects a profound understanding of family as both a gift and a responsibility. For those of us crafting our narratives, we must consider how our faith and experiences can shape the upbringing of our own children and influence the larger community.

To inspire future generations, we need to be deliberate in sharing our stories, especially the aspects that exemplify growth through struggle. Each woman in the Bible teaches us that vulnerabilities can be pillars of strength. Miriam, for instance, displayed courage as she led Israel in worship after crossing the Red Sea. Her defiance against oppression and her strength as a leader during a tumultuous time teach us the critical importance of standing firm in our beliefs. As mothers, friends, and mentors, we have a responsibility to instill these lessons of courage and faith in our children, reminding them that it is not only acceptable to stand up for what is right but also imperative.

Ruth's narrative introduces us to the themes of loyalty and resilience against the backdrop of adversity. Her choice to remain with Naomi, a foreigner in a strange land, highlights the importance of familial bonds and loyalty in ensuring survival amid hardship. Ruth's story encourages us to cherish the relationships in our lives and to stand by one another through thick and thin. As we cultivate relationships with the youth among us, we must demonstrate the value of loyalty and the strength found in community. The wisdom passed down from Ruth encourages future generations to forge connections built on trust and compassion, further defining their identities.

Esther's boldness in the face of danger provides another essential lesson. Her willingness to risk her life to save her people underscores the reality that sometimes we must take decisive action for the greater good. Drawing from Esther's bravery reminds us that future generations need role models who exemplify moral courage, who inspire them to act when faced with injustice. As we share her story, we can highlight scenarios in our own lives where we faced difficult choices, how we navigated them, and the outcomes borne from those decisions. How we respond to injustice, whether through our voices or our actions, leaves an indelible mark on those who witness our lives.

The act of storytelling also serves as a tool for emotional connection and transformation. Sharing our struggles, triumphs, and the lessons gleaned from our experiences invites others into a space of empathy and understanding. When we narrate our own stories, not only do we offer insight into our journeys, but we also extend an invitation to engage with the complexities of human experience. People find strength in vulnerability, and the ability to relate to the trials faced by others can inspire hope and resilience in times of difficulty. In our testimonies, we can incorporate the virtues highlighted by these biblical women, presenting them not just as historical figures but as relatable mentors. It is essential to reinforce to our children and peers that these lessons were not confined to a particular time or culture; they resonate through time and invite us to live them out now.

Consider the ordinary moments of life where lessons surface. A simple act of kindness or a moment of sacrifice can reverberate through generations. Recounting these experiences enriches our narratives and allows us to frame our lives within the wider context of these timeless teachings. The responsibility of inspiring future generations requires us to remain actively engaged in our stories, continuously reflecting on the lessons learned and how we communicate them.

As women, as storytellers, and as leaders within our families and communities, we must intentionally cultivate an environment where the achievements and challenges faced by those who came before us are acknowledged and celebrated. Our legacy is not merely about preserving history; it is about actively contributing to the narrative of those who will come after us. By sharing our stories and the lessons they contain, we nurture the soil from which future growth will arise.

We should also consider that our legacy inevitably intertwines with our faith. Across the stories of Hannah, Miriam, Ruth, and Esther, we see the steadfastness of faith – in God's promise, in community, and in one another. Faith is a powerful thread that connects generations, providing a foundation upon which we can build our unique stories. We can encourage future generations to embrace their faith as a source of strength, guiding them through life's challenges and shaping their responses to the world around them.

In nurturing the next generation, a reciprocal exchange occurs. The stories we share may empower others to reclaim their own narratives, to see themselves as authors of their destinies. Assuring young women that their voices matter, just like those of the women we've studied, will inspire them to stand confidently in their truth. We must encourage them to see their experiences as valuable lessons that can contribute to the collective legacy of womanhood.

Moreover, as we inspire future generations, we should not shy away from the tough conversations necessary for growth. Addressing issues like injustice, gender equality, and mental health with honesty fosters a space for growth and healing. Sharing our struggles with these realities can help others feel less alone. This openness allows younger generations to grapple with complex feelings as they navigate their own lives, equipping them with the tools they need to advocate for themselves and others.

Encouraging dialogue about faith, hope, and resilience will help cultivate characteristics in future generations that mirror those seen in the stories of biblical women. Discussions about dreams, aspirations, and the importance of community can reinforce a sense of possibility. When young men and women hear stories of strong women who overcame adversity, it instills confidence in their capacity to shape their own stories. Each conversation plants seeds of hope and encourages curiosity, a crucial element for budding leaders.

As we seek to inspire future generations, we must remain aware of the medium through which our stories reach them. In our digital age, the methods of storytelling have evolved significantly. Our narratives can now traverse vast distances through a screen, making access to our collective experiences easier than ever before. Utilizing social media platforms, blogs, or podcasts allows us to share lessons from our lives and the lives of those who came before us with a broader audience.

In harnessing technology, we stay connected, transforming traditional storytelling into interactive sessions that engage our listeners on multiple levels. The power of visual stories and shared experiences can resonate with youth in ways that traditional narratives may not. By employing a blend of storytelling and modern communication, we can reach young hearts and minds, captivating their attention and igniting their imaginations.

It is equally essential to model the values we wish to instill. Children learn more from what they observe than from what they are told. As we navigate our lives with intention, embodying principles of faith, resilience, and courage, we not only honor the legacy of those women in Scripture but also illuminate the path for the next generation. Our actions – how we treat others, how we respond to challenges, and how we remain faithful – serve as lessons they will internalize.

Ultimately, inspiring future generations is a multi-faceted responsibility. It transcends mere storytelling and extends into action, reflection, and engagement. As we gather the threads of legacy from the stories of biblical women, we must weave them into our own lives, letting their lessons inform our decisions, interactions, and the narratives we continue to craft.

As we conclude this exploration of our responsibility to inspire future generations, let us remember the impact of a single story. Each woman whose tale graces the pages of Scripture has left us with invaluable teachings that resonate across time. By integrating those lessons into our lives, sharing them openly, and embodying the principles they represent, we stand poised to ignite passion and purpose in those who follow us. Through our stories, we have the power to inspire a new generation, encouraging them to embrace their identities, forge their paths, and contribute to the beautiful tapestry of shared humanity. Our stories are not only ours; they are the threads that will weave the future, and we have the exhilarating opportunity to fill that canvas with truth, light, and love.

CONCLUSION: THANKS FOR TAKING THIS JOURNEY WITH ME

Hey, Awesome Readers!

Wow, can you believe we have reached the end? What an amazing journey it's been! As we wrap up this exploration into lessons from women of the Bible, I want to take a moment to pause, reflect, and be grateful. Thank you for sharing this journey with me; your presence has made every word spark a little brighter!

I hope you've found inspiration hopping off these pages like a joyous rabbit in a field of daisies. Whether you saw a glimmer of light or a rush of ideas explode in your mind, I'm thrilled you took this leap with me! Remember, the energy we have cultivated together doesn't stop here. It's a catalyst for more, and I urge you to take these insights, play with them, and let them blossom in your own unique way.

Don't just close this book and pack it away; carry that spark with you into your everyday life. Wake up tomorrow and embark on your own adventure! Write that story, create that art, or start that project you've been putting off. Your creative potential is boundless, like the vast sky above us, just waiting for you to reach for the stars!

I genuinely believe that learning does not have a finish line; it's a continuous journey filled with thrilling twists and unexpected turns. So let's promise each other to keep the flame alive, to nurture our ideas, and to rejoice in the process of creation! I encourage you to share your experiences, your successes, and even the face-plants along the way. Let's build a community of fearless seekers who lift one another up!

As we part ways, don't forget that the real fun starts when you embrace your unique voice and let it shine brightly. May your path be filled with color, light, and endless possibilities! Here's to inspiration; may it fuel your heart and light up the world around you!

With much gratitude to God,

Rev. Dr. Claudette C. Rodney

www.ingramcontent.com/pod-product-compliance
Lightning Source LLC
Chambersburg PA
CBHW041030050726
47599CB00018B/1915